RESIDENT, INTERRUPTED

By Ashley Kate Bourne, DO

Published January 20, 2026 by Praxis House Press

For Tyler: thank you for being there with me on every single page. I would not have made it to the end of the book without you.

In college, I volunteered on an inpatient psychiatric unit, expecting to observe from a safe distance. Instead, I found myself sitting beside patients who trusted me with the rawest parts of their stories. One afternoon, a teenager described the weight of her depression as if she were narrating someone else's life—flat, distant, exhausted. I remember listening as the psychiatrist joined us, watching how he spoke to her with respect and gentleness, and how her guarded posture softened within minutes.

I didn't know the terminology then. I couldn't yet distinguish affect from mood or understand the nuances of diagnosis. But I recognized what I was witnessing: the transformative power of being seen. That moment stayed with me long after I left the unit.

In his book, *The Last Lecture,* Randy Pausch writes, "Experience is what you get when you didn't get what you wanted. And experience is often the most valuable thing you have to offer." Experience was what I got when I didn't match in psychiatry and instead accepted a transitional year residency position. That experience, though initially disappointing, turned out to be exactly what I needed: a chance to hone my diagnostic skills, work as a physician for a year, treat patients in numerous specialties, and reaffirm that psychiatry is my calling.

Through my work as a resident in these first months since graduation, I've come to realize a renewed passion for mental health. I always make it a point to ask my patients how they are feeling, not just physically, but also mentally. While hospitalized, many patients see their mental health deteriorate at an alarming rate . Constant IV pump alarms, nighttime blood draws that interrupt sleep, and an overload of medical jargon can all be detrimental to a patient who needs quiet time to heal. As a resident, I've provided my patients with a listening ear, allowing them to share their stories and ask questions about their condition. At the end of the day, connecting with my patients and being part of the reason they feel better is what's most important to me.

Soon after accepting my transitional year spot, I began my final medical school rotation in child and adolescent psychiatry with a doctor I had worked with before. Despite knowing my dream of becoming a psychiatrist had been put on hold for a year, I rediscovered my love for the specialty.

Towards the end of my rotation, I had a patient, "Emilio," who had been through unspeakable trauma with his adoptive parents and was now back in the foster care system. Faced with an unstable living situation and working through his past trauma, Emilio started drinking alcohol on a daily basis. I worked with Emilio daily for a week, and though I only made a small dent in his overall progress, I saw improvement in his outlook and mood over that week. Upon discharging Emilio, I knew I wanted to dedicate my career to patients like him: those who have no one in their corner fighting for them. Now that I am three months into residency, I know that the clinical expertise I am gaining, now and in the future, will serve to help me become the psychiatrist I am meant to be.

Early psychiatric screening and intervention has saved so many people from a lifetime of struggles and inpatient hospitalization. Currently, we live in a society where there are more patients in need of psychiatric care than psychiatrists who are trained to provide that care. As a psychiatrist, I hope to equip my patients with the tools they need to manage their conditions and to build lasting partnerships that honor their unique circumstances. While I'll never be able to help every patient, I hope that those lives I do touch are forever changed for the better.

The words you just read are lifted straight from my personal statement—the carefully polished essay every fourth-year medical student writes in hopes of convincing a residency program director to take a chance on them. But what comes next isn't polished. It's messy, raw, and sometimes uncomfortable. This is the story behind the essay—the depression, the failures, the quiet humiliations, the moments of grace.

Residency is supposed to be the culmination of everything you've worked toward in medicine: the sleepless nights studying, the board exams that left your eyes burning, the endless patient notes written as a student when no one really needed them. Residency is the moment you finally become a doctor in more than name only.

At least, that's the story we tell.

The truth is messier. Residency is both a beginning and a breaking. It's a crucible that takes the brightest, most idealistic young doctors and presses until something cracks. Sometimes what cracks is arrogance. Sometimes it's resilience. Sometimes it's your mental health. For me, it was all three.

I didn't write this book because my path is extraordinary. I wrote it because I know it isn't. Every resident carries their own quiet griefs: the patient they still have nightmares about, the shift that broke them, the diagnosis that came too late, the day they questioned whether they belonged in medicine at all. What I offer here is my version of that story—one psychiatrist-in-training stumbling through the fire, sometimes burning, sometimes rising from the ashes.

If you're a medical student, maybe this will prepare you. If you're a patient, maybe this will show you the human being behind the white coat. If you've never set foot in a hospital, maybe this will remind you that the people who care for you are not immune to needing care themselves.

This isn't the version of my life you'd find in an application packet or hear in an interview. It's the version with the cracks showing—the story of how residency broke me, and how I began to put myself back together.

Listen as you read

Each part of this book opens with the songs that carried me through that season of residency. They weren't just background music, they were lifelines. You'll find the playlists at the start of each section, and the full collection is available through the QR codes below.

Apple Music

Spotify

PART ONE

BREAKING

These songs are for the collapse—the unmatched email, the fog of depression, the shame you can't quite put words to. They sound like isolation, like walking through the world on autopilot. This was the soundtrack of everything unraveling.

1. "this is me trying" by—Taylor Swift
2. "Scott Street" by—Phoebe Bridgers
3. "Liability" by—Lorde
4. "Breathe Me" by—Sia
5. "The Archer" by—Taylor Swift
6. "What Was I Made For?" by—Billie Eilish
7. "Torn" by Natalie Imbruglia

CHAPTER ONE

Reflections on Going Unmatched—a Year Later

March 11, 2024: the worst day of my medical career. I opened an email from the National Residency Match Program (NRMP) that said, "We are sorry, you did not match any position," and my hopes and dreams were immediately crushed.

I was sitting cross-legged on the couch, laptop balanced on my knees, the late-morning light spilling through the blinds in uneven stripes. My two best friends were on FaceTime and my fiancé, Tyler, was beside me, anxiously waiting to find out where we would be moving to in a few short months. When the email popped up, I clicked without thinking—expecting nerves, maybe relief, but not this.

The words blurred instantly: *We are sorry, you did not match any position.* For a moment, the room felt impossibly still, like the air had been sucked out. I heard the faint hum of the refrigerator in the kitchen, the muted tick of the ceiling fan, and underneath it, my own breath quickening. Tyler looked at me, eyebrows drawn, already preparing for the flood of emotions that were about to come. He saw the tears before they rolled down my cheeks and he hung up on my friends—they had just received *good* news, and we needed to mourn this alone before we shared it with them. But they already knew. My face betrayed me.

All I remember is this: the weight of Tyler's arm pulling me against him, my laptop sliding to the floor with a muted thud, the warm tears streaming down my face and landing on my chest. All I could think was *this can't be happening*—over and over, like a skipping record—until the words became meaningless noise in my head.

And then, beneath the disbelief sat shame. Hot, prickling, and so much heavier than I'd imagined it could be.

I had spent the previous four years working towards this day—the Monday of Match week—only to have my dreams crushed in an instant. As a fourth-year medical student, I stood on the precipice of the rest of my career as a physician. I would still graduate, but I would not be starting residency in the specialty of my choice: psychiatry.

Because there are thousands of students who don't match each year, there's a program called supplemental offer and acceptance program (SOAP). Basically, all of the residency programs in the country open their spots to all of the unmatched med students, and there is a scramble to try and fill those positions. Prior to that fateful Monday, I had always looked down on those who had to go through SOAP, borne out of that quiet superiority that is all too common in medicine. I thought that I was better than that, that I could never need to do it because surely a residency program would want *me!* I'd soon learn how very wrong I was.

SOAP starts one hour after the dreaded "we are sorry" email goes out. Meaning I had sixty minutes to cry, scream, then get my life together before putting on a brave face. My mom came down to Miami to share the moment with me—whether that meant celebrating or, as it turned out, going through all the programs with open spots, typing into a shared note on our phones, and working on my mission: I would have a job by the end of the week.

The next few days were a blur of two dozen phone interviews with residency program directors. I applied broadly to multiple specialties: family and internal medicine, emergency medicine, pediatrics, and transitional year programs. Each phone call was an unannounced formal-ish interview—I had to smile my way through the pain, pacing around our apartment as I tried to sell myself to these doctors. I lied through my teeth, saying, *yes, I applied to psychiatry, but I've had a change of heart, and my real dream is to be a primary care doctor.* It didn't feel good, changing myself to fit the version they wanted to see, but it had to be done. When you graduate from medical school, you hold a doctorate degree, but you aren't qualified to work as a doctor without residency training. Each specialist (or generalist) must go through their respective residency to be a qualified physician in the field of their choice. I'd have to wait a year to reapply for psychiatry, but I was doing the only thing I could: move forward. Each night, I went to bed feeling a tiny bit better about my situation.

A few days later, I received three offers from residency programs: two transitional years and one pediatrics program. I chose to accept an offer from one of the transitional year programs, which was local and enabled Tyler to keep his job.

Tyler and I went out to "celebrate" my job. We went to a local Italian restaurant, and I wore my favorite dress, trying to display myself as the confident young doctor I would soon be.

I was acting.

Little did I know how much acting I would be doing in the year ahead. Our dinner together wasn't a Match Day celebration at all—it was the opposite. I had scrambled into a position I didn't really want. I was grateful for it, and so was Tyler, who had been carrying us financially through medical school, but the excitement never came. I plastered on a smile and played the part of being fine when I was anything but. My dream of psychiatry had been shoved onto a shelf for another year. I wasn't okay, or happy, or content. I was livid, disappointed, and embarrassed.

I ordered the fettuccine Alfredo and enjoyed a lovely apricot cocktail. I decided to pass on dessert, but not before I posted the ultimate fake Instagram story: a shot of our glasses clinking in celebration, with the text *celebrating my first doctor job!* in small font in the corner. Understated, like my feelings about the whole thing.

A week later, I turned twenty-six. We took the day off to drive to my parents' house for wedding business: getting our marriage license, sampling cake flavors, and tasting our reception menu. It should have been pure joy, and in some ways it was. I do look back on that day fondly, but under the laughter and frosting samples was a heaviness I couldn't shake.

Another week passed, and the sadness still hadn't lifted. One night after a shower, I found myself curled on the cold bathroom tile, sobbing into a damp towel. From the living room, Monday Night Football blared, the announcers' voices masking my cries. Tyler eventually noticed I'd been gone too long. When he found me in a heap on the floor, his face fell, then he shifted into caretaker mode. He lifted me up, dried my cheeks, and helped me into pajamas. He guided me to the couch, muted the TV, and turned to face me fully.

We talked. About how unfair this was, how angry and disappointed I felt, and how different our year was going to look. And then he asked the simplest question: *What can I do to make it easier?* We began to piece together a plan—not to erase the disappointment, but to survive it together.

Fast forward to July 1 of that year: the notorious day when all medical interns start their jobs at the hospital. Since that fateful day in March, I had graduated medical school, gotten married, and gone on my honeymoon to Italy. Then, I started on an inpatient internal medicine rotation, also known as the hospitalist service. We admitted patients, placed consults to subspecialties, managed heart failure, pneumonia, and other common presentations, and discharged patients back home or to nursing facilities. To be frank, I hated that job. I still had that new-grad giddiness—I was a doctor! I was finally doing the job that I had studied for my entire adult life. However, the work itself was largely unfulfilling.

The downside (or upside) to my transitional year program was that

I would have to reapply to psychiatry in the next cycle. That meant that while I did not enjoy my internal medicine job, I at least had the opportunity to change my fate—with a lot of work. Applying to residency is no joke. It requires a personal statement (a one-page essay that proves to residency programs that you are a good person and well-suited for the specialty you're applying to), multiple letters of recommendation from physicians in that specialty, and innumerable volunteer, research, and extracurricular activities. Once you get through the first stage, next come the interviews. I reapplied to psychiatry and family medicine as a "backup" specialty (because I could not cope with the horror of not matching again), which meant I had double the number of interviews. In September and October, I completed ten interviews and scheduled fifteen more.

October 31, 2024: I was four months into being a doctor (and still not loving it). I had an interview for a psychiatry residency, which ended with an offer I wouldn't dream of passing up: a second-year residency spot starting in July 2025. This was the best possible outcome of my nightmare year. I was thrilled! I accepted it within the hour, consulting only my husband and my mom when making my decision. Finally, I had a spot to train as a psychiatrist, and at the same institution where I completed my undergraduate degree.

The rest of my intern year was a blur, 65-plus hour work weeks combined with the worst depression I've ever experienced. During the latter half of the year, I was blessed (or more aptly, cursed) with three straight months of inpatient medicine—six-day work weeks, ten-to-twelve- hour days, and constant work.

I felt like I was buried and could never dig my way out.

I restarted the antidepressant I hadn't taken for over a year and confided in family and friends regarding the severity of my depression. My mental health as a fourth-year medical student—prior to not matching—was honestly really good. I was in my final year of medical school, one of the most grueling things a twenty-something can put themselves through, and I was proud of myself.

During the week of SOAP, the depression hit me hard, but having to pull myself together for my birthday a week later and our wedding the following month, I was able to cover up the sadness by celebrating things that made me truly happy. During intern year, on my *one* sacred day off each week, my anhedonia (the inability to enjoy things that are usually pleasurable, like reading, for me) manifested as staying in bed until 4:00 p.m., barely eating, and absolutely no social plans. It was a harrowing time.

I had never imagined that my intern year would look so bleak.

Here's the thing about depression: when you're in the throes of it, it feels like you can never escape it, but suddenly, the fog lifts! Life is worth living again! It's almost surprising how quickly your life can change for the better when you're living in that fog. Fortunately, a combination of the antidepressant and therapy pulled me out of my funk. I felt like myself again, and I could not be more thankful. I finished up my intern year—those awful months of inpatient medicine did end—and I made the move with my husband to our new city for my psychiatry residency. For the first time in a long time, I had a renewed sense of hope for my future.

Now, I am one month into my second year of residency and psychiatry training. These past thirty-one days have been filled with learning, meaningful connections with coworkers, and fulfilling work. As a second-year resident, I get to do one half-day per week in the adult outpatient psychiatry clinic, and those Monday afternoons have become my favorite thing.

I feel as if I have found my calling.

As I enter my second month of psychiatry residency, I am filled with hope and excitement for the career ahead of me.

If I could go back and speak to the woman I was on Match Day, I would tell her that while it won't be easy, you will get through it, and you will be so much stronger for it. The days will be long, but intern year will be short. There will be times when you don't want to wake up and do it all, but you'll do it anyway, and that will make you into the most resilient version of yourself.

To anyone going through a dark time right now, know that it is temporary, and the sunshine feels so much warmer once the clouds clear. I'm thankful to be living in the sun right now, but I know that when the clouds come back, I can handle it.

Here's the thing about going unmatched that no one says out loud: there is *so much shame.* My first feeling after opening that dreaded email from the NRMP was disappointment, but about a second later, all I felt was shame.

Regardless of your career, imagine this: you work for eight years towards a specific goal (the length of an undergraduate degree followed immediately by four years of medical school, assuming you did not take a gap year to strengthen your resume), and on the day you are "chosen" for that goal, you're left out. It's like being back in third grade gym class and nobody wants you on their team. It was as if they were saying, *you're not good enough. We don't believe in you. This dream is not meant for you. Try something else.*

How does one recover from that shame? How do you build yourself back up to a point where you have confidence again?

I don't know that I have the perfect answer to that question, but I can tell you what I did. I faked it 'til I made it, because that's all I *could* do. Though I hated it, I showed up each day of my intern year. At the time, I could barely admit to myself how much I hated it. There was a small part of me that thought, *well, I guess this is what being a doctor is like. This is what I studied for, and this is just how it is ... and the fact that I hate it is a reflection of me and my poor judgement in choosing to go to medical school.*

But I can happily report that as a psychiatry resident, I do not hate being a doctor. In fact, I love it and feel that I have found the only job in the world I am truly meant for.

Unfortunately, for the entirety of intern year, I had to put on a brave face and pretend to like my job. That was no easy feat—being a resident is a mentally demanding job that requires you to show up every morning as your best self, ready to care for the sickest patients.

So, how did I do it? How do you gaslight yourself into thinking that you actually want to do a job that you hate?

You don't.

In the coming pages, I'll delve into how intern year broke me, but let's try to focus on the positives for a minute, because it wasn't all bad. I had experiences during my intern year that I truly loved and am so grateful for. One of those is the month I spent in critical care medicine, working in the intensive care unit (ICU).

I showed up on my first day in the ICU and knew immediately that I needed to befriend the nurses. As a brand-new baby intern doctor, I did not know how to keep ICU patients alive on my own. But you know who did ? The *nurses.* That first day I went right up to each of them and introduced myself. I was honest, admitting that I felt like a fish out of water, and that I would appreciate any feedback they could offer. I acknowledged that each of them had years more experience than I did, and I would never be able to do my job without their help. Turns out, kindness and honesty go a long way! I firmly believe that in getting the nurses on my side from day one, my month in the ICU was significantly more successful than it would have been otherwise.

Something you need to know about an ICU patient: they have about a dozen things going on at once. Their heart is failing, their volume overloaded, but at the same time, their blood pressure is dropping. With that, they also have labile blood sugars, which are difficult to control, intense pain, and a liver that is struggling to metabolize all of the drugs we are constantly infusing. One patient alone would take hours to analyze and come up with a plan. Trouble was, I had five patients per day, not just one. Relying on the nurses was a lifeline for me.

I had a few patients in the ICU who have stuck with me, but there is one in particular I still think about. He was an elderly gentleman with a large family, a devoted wife and several loving daughters who were at his bedside day and night. I first met this patient, who I'll refer to as "Pat," when he was coding on the regular medical floor. Coding is a term used in healthcare to refer to cardiac arrest requiring CPR. When a patient "codes," the hospital will call a "code blue" and the ICU team goes running to the patient's room. CPR begins, epinephrine is given via IV, and sometimes we will deliver a shock to the patient's heart.

Pat coded. Twice.

After the second time in as many hours, he was intubated and transferred to the ICU, where I assumed his care. I could tell immediately that he was very sick. He was in his eighties and had lived a long and seemingly happy life. His wife, who was sobbing when I first met her, was healthier than her husband and not quite ready to give up her life with him. As Pat's hospital stay wore on, I noticed his wife coming to terms with her new reality: Pat would not be leaving the hospital and going back to his normal life. *If* he were able to leave, he would require long-term acute care at a nursing facility. Pat's wife quickly realized this was not what she wanted for him, and not what he would have wanted for himself. Ultimately, the decision was made to place Pat on do not resuscitate (DNR). This meant that if his heart were to stop, we would not provide CPR, and instead would allow him to pass peacefully.

The day that Pat and his family made that decision, I felt myself becoming emotional. It was beautiful to see his wife hug him and read his eyes without needing to exchange words. They both knew this was the end for Pat, but it was the end of a beautiful marriage, which resulted in four daughters, all of whom stood by his bedside until the last moment.

I wondered—would his family judge me for crying when I said goodbye at the end of my shift, knowing that I likely would not see him again the next day? I worried his family would be offended if I showed my emotion. I thought that by expressing sadness they might feel I was *stealing* their sadness, that it wasn't my family member to be sad about.

To this day, I'm not sure if his family saw me tearing up as I said goodbye. I hope that if they did, they knew it came from a place of love and caring. I was immensely grateful for the opportunity to care for Pat and to help his family come to their decision regarding palliative care (care provided in the final phase of a terminal illness).

My experience with Pat was not a unique one. There were many patients and families during that month in the ICU where I had to have discussions about palliative care versus continued aggressive treatment. These discussions were challenging but necessary.

I was reminded of a book I read in college: *Being Mortal* by Atul Gawande. In his book, which is a stunning exploration of human mortality, he emphasizes advance directives. An advance directive, sometimes known as a living will, outlines what you would want during the last stages of your life when you are no longer capable of making your own medical decisions. In an advance directive, you can dictate whether you would want to be intubated and mechanically ventilated, how aggressive you would want to be with treatment, and much more. It allows you to control your care when you're incapacitated.

There was no moment in intern year that made me more aware of my mortality than my month in the ICU. Compared to my previous months of residency, when I felt like I had to gaslight myself into believing I liked being a doctor, I actually *did* like it. It made me feel like I was doing meaningful work and impressed upon me the importance of writing an advance directive so that you can live your final days the way you want. Dying with dignity is not something everyone gets—but it is something we all deserve.

CHAPTER TWO

Intern Year and How It Broke Me

I mentioned in the first part of this book that my intern year brought with it some of the most severe depression I've ever experienced, and that is no lie.

If you've never been depressed before, you might not know what it looks like, so let me paint a picture of a typical day: you finally wake up after snoozing your alarm three times, which allows you the bare minimum amount of time needed to get dressed and brush your teeth. The only reason you're able to get up from your slumber is because the fear of losing everything you've worked towards is greater than your desire to rot in bed all day. You're looking like you just rolled out of bed (because you did), but you don't care. As long as you show up to work, that's all that matters, right? You drive to work in silence because even your favorite music can't cheer you up. After arriving at the hospital, you walk like a zombie to the resident workroom, log into the computer, and start chart reviewing your patients for the day. You work for an hour or so, then your grumbling stomach and burgeoning headache prompt you to walk down to the cafeteria for breakfast. You grab a bagel and a Gatorade. You gave up drinking energy drinks a few months ago because they were making your anxiety exponentially worse. You scarf down the bagel and make your way upstairs to pre-round on all your patients.

While speaking to them, you plaster on a smile that you hope seems genuine, because what's worse than being sick in the hospital than being sick in the hospital *and* having a doctor that is overtly depressed. You see all ten of your patients, which takes longer than you want it to because they all want to chat and you don't have the heart to stop them. You show up for rounds with the rest of the team, and they're all cheerily discussing their weekend plans. You paste on a fake smile and nod while they chat, contributing nothing because your "weekend plans" are to go to work one day, and to sleep all day the next. Rounds go by without much incident, and you take detailed notes on the plan for each patient based on what the attending physician wants. You join the other residents for lunch in the cafeteria, but again, sit quietly as they talk animatedly about whatever new TV show they're binging, or the restaurant in town they want to check out together. It doesn't matter because you won't be joining them.

The rest of the afternoon passes in a blur, you finish your notes, you drink copious amounts of water, and you look at the clock way too often. Finally, it's 5:30 p.m. and you're free to go home. But suddenly, you don't want to confront the sadness you know will engulf you when you get there. You dilly-dally, chatting idly with other residents before finally walking to the parking garage.

Again, you drive in silence. You consider calling your mom to talk about your day but know that she will sense the depression in your voice. You arrive home and walk inside, where your dog greets you with unapologetic joy. Briefly, life feels worth living again, but then he calms down and your mood falls back.

Your husband isn't home from work yet, so you make a quick dinner of mostly snacks just so that you can say you ate. You shower and get in bed, where your thoughts immediately sink even lower—you feel as if you'd be better off dead.

You don't actually want to *do anything* … but you wish that maybe you'd die suddenly in your sleep or get in a fatal car accident on the way to work. This is what we call *passive suicidal ideation*—not making any preparations, not writing a suicide note, but just going about your day, hoping that something might end everything for you. You've seen patients in medical school who experienced passive suicidal ideation, but despite this expertise, you're powerless when it comes to stopping the thoughts.

Eventually, your husband gets home and tucks you in, then you close your crying eyes and attempt to fall asleep. It takes hours, but after a while the tears on your cheeks dry, and you drift into an uneasy sleep.

And the next day, you do it all over again.

And again.

And again.

The whole day, and the weeks on end of days that look like that, makes you feel numb. There were no emotions, only going through the motions that I knew were expected of me—by my husband, by my colleagues, and by the system of residency.

I'm sure you can imagine how those days got old and drove me to feel even more suicidal. *That* is what intern year did to me. The three months straight of inpatient medicine felt insurmountable to me, and I dug myself into a hole I felt I could never climb my way out of.

So, we've established that intern year broke me, but obviously something put me back together because I'm writing these words now, several months later. The three things that put me back together were an SSRI, therapy, and support from friends and family. As a psychiatrist, I am the first person to admit that sometimes medication just does not help enough. But I am fortunate that escitalopram *saved me*. I had taken Lexapro in the past, starting in high school and through college, but was not currently on it when the intern-year depression hit hard. Luckily, I was able to get a prescription quickly and restart my medication, and I am so thankful I did. After seeing patients devolve quickly into full fledged depression requiring hospitalization, I knew that I had to do *something* to take a step towards getting better.

SSRIs don't work quickly. The literature agrees they take three to four weeks to reach maximum blood levels to be effective. When you're in the deep hole of depression, three to four weeks feels like a very long time. However, I think there is an element of hope when you start these medications: you know that you are doing *something* to help your mental health, and if you just keep doing it, one day soon, maybe you won't be so sad anymore.

I credit Lexapro and therapy for saving my life during intern year— but more on that later.

CHAPTER THREE
Tiny Acts of Rebellion Against an Oppressive System

One thing that residency teaches you is to *live for the weekend*. But you can't—if you only allow yourself to thrive on the days that you're not spending in the hospital, you're letting the job win. You're letting medicine take over your life and limiting yourself to real happiness and fulfillment on the rare days off. In many residencies, you only have one day off per week or every other weekend off (these are 6:1 or 12:2 models, respectively). Frankly, they both suck. There's a reason the rest of the working world only sits at their desks Monday through Friday from 9 a.m. to 5 p.m.: because 60-plus-hour work weeks (the norm in residency!) are not sustainable.

During my intern year—which we have established, was extremely depressing—I lived for the weekends, until I wasn't living at all. By stacking all my "life stuff" on my one day off per week (my program followed a 6:1 model), I created excessive pressure for that single day to be perfect. And more often than not, it wasn't, because life gets in the way.

For example, I would plan my weekend day as follows: sleep in (to 8:00 or 9:00 a.m.), go grocery shopping, meet a friend for coffee, vacuum and mop the entire house, do laundry, create content for Instagram, read a book, watch a movie with my husband, exercise, take an "everything shower," and maybe have a date night. If you're thinking that that sounds like too much for one day, that's because it was! Inevitably, there was a part of me that began to dread this day off—it was so overwhelming to *have* to do all those household tasks, "fun" things, and general life maintenance all in one day.

As intern year wore on, and my weekend day grew more and more daunting, I started to give up.

I let the depression win.

Instead of being proactive on my day off, I did nothing, and I mean *nothing*. I would fall asleep late on Friday night, doomscrolling on

TikTok until my eyelids grew heavy, then I would wake after a fitful sleep to an empty home (my husband frequently worked on weekends). Without him as a witness to my rotting, I would stay in bed. All day.

Around 4:00 p.m. I'd emerge from the cave of our dark bedroom (thanks to my early investment in blackout curtains for when I was on night shift) and go downstairs. Still in my pajamas, I would eat my first food of the day. Usually something easily digestible, like a banana with peanut butter. After supplying my ever-shrinking body with some caloric sustenance, I'd return to my bedroom to doomscroll some more.

The saddest part—well, it was all sad—was how my hobbies receded into nothingness. You would think that a resident physician with one day off per week would fill her free time with her favorite things, but no. For me, my favorite thing is reading.

In med school, I read an average of fifty books per year, totaling well over two hundred for the four years I studied. I was proud of myself for maintaining that hobby throughout school. Many people, including my mom, told me I would not be able to keep it up: "how could you possibly read a book per week *and* study for hours on end?" she'd ask. I did it though!

I learned that in order to keep my sanity in medical school, I *had* to keep reading. It was my escape from the reality of studying histology slides, drug mechanisms, and disease classifications. Without reading, I would've succumbed to depression in medical school. Instead, I put off the dark cloud of depression until residency.

Losing interest in my hobbies (or hobby, since really, it's just reading), otherwise known as anhedonia, was one of the most prominent symptoms of my depression. As a psychiatrist, I originally learned the symptoms of depression as the mnemonic SIGECAPS—sleep, interest, guilt, energy, concentration, appetite, psychomotor, and suicide. I could elaborate on all of those, but for now let's suffice it to say that I had symptoms from every single category. And many of them would manifest on my day off, as I've shown.

In sum, my intern year started with me living for the weekend (or my one-day version of it) and ended by my not living at all. I let residency win. But in my second year of residency, I turned that around.

The alternative to living for the weekend is doing what I hope most people do—live every day. What I mean by that is this: your work friends invite you out for drinks on Monday after work. You say yes! Why not? You didn't have any plans other than sitting at home with your husband, eating pasta and watching jeopardy, and you've got the rest of your lives to do that. On Tuesday, you go to a workout class at your favorite gym after work. Sweating is a form of medicine, after all. On Wednesday, you have book club with your co-residents, which you organized. Everyone meets at your house and you enjoy a potluck of snacks while discussing the book you all read. On Thursday, you and your husband go out to a Thai restaurant for date night. And on Friday, you go to dinner with a group of friends.

While this example may be a bit extreme, the sentiment is that instead of forcing yourself only to enjoy life on the weekend, you do something every weekday (or at least most weekdays) that brings you joy. That is not to say that working on the weekdays isn't fulfilling, but honestly, work is just a job. Even in medicine, though society expects us to be so devoted to our careers that we literally forgo having a social life for years on end, being a doctor is a job that pays the bills. And sidebar—in residency, it barely pays the bills! But that's a conversation for another day (or perhaps another chapter).

During my second year of residency, I was very intentional about my social life. After barely seeing my med school friends during intern year, and making absolutely zero effort to make new friends in my transitional year program, I was determined to change that in my second year. From week one, I said yes more. I went to trivia night at the brewery on Tuesdays. I did, in fact, start a book club within my residency! My husband and I brought back weekly date nights— something we had been religious about when we were dating and engaged. All these little things added up to make a happier life. It also took the pressure off my weekends. Instead of feeling like I had to do everything on my day (or days) off, (as a psychiatry resident, I got at least two *full weekends off* per month … what a treat) I crammed a lot into my social calendar on the weekdays. This left my weekends free for other things, like grocery shopping and cleaning the house, or just doing nothing for a change. And unlike during intern year when doing nothing was a literal symptom of depression (we call it psychomotor depression in the business), doing nothing for a couple of hours on a Saturday in my second year just meant I needed more time to recharge. I was doing *so much* during the week that I allowed myself to truly rest on the weekend. What a concept!

Not letting residency win and living on the weekdays *as well as* the weekend is an example of a tiny act of rebellion against the system that is graduate medical education. In doing so, I was not compromising my work ethic or the quality of my patient care, but I was doing something for myself that didn't let residency have 100 percent control over my life. There are other tiny acts of rebellion that I've enacted throughout my time as a trainee, which are like small little middle fingers to the bureaucratic system in place—it's my way of saying "you can't win."

CHAPTER FOUR

The Physical Impact of Depression and Burnout

I mentioned earlier the mnemonic we use in psychiatry to check for symptoms of depression: SIGECAPS. Many of those symptoms—namely sleep, energy, appetite, and psychomotor—are physical rather than mental or emotional. When I struggled with depression as an intern, I had problems in all four domains.

Sleep: this was likely the root of my depression. During my emergency medicine rotation, my anxiety was through the roof. I would come home from work and cry. The day had been so overwhelming with constant noise, overstimulation, and the feeling of being an off-service resident who had no idea what she was doing. I felt more like a hindrance than a help to the attending physicians. This sensation crushed my people-pleasing nature—side note: find me a doctor who isn't a people-pleaser at heart, I bet you can't—and left me feeling woefully inadequate. Cue every doctor's worst friend: imposter syndrome. My month in the ER was the beginning of the downward slope for my mental health.

There was one night after a particularly loud shift—beeps, code blues, yelling patients—when I slept for exactly one hour and fourteen minutes. That's it. Imagine going to the ER and being cared for by a resident who not only felt like a horrific doctor but also slept less than the length of a movie. It wasn't safe, and I'm not proud of it. I tried to compensate by being more cautious and conservative, checking everything with my attending, but the truth is that no one can practice well in that state.

Driving to work after so little sleep was never wise, but in residency, it was expected. The irony was hard to ignore: the lounge walls were plastered with flyers about burnout and exhaustion, warning us not to drive or care for patients while sleep deprived. And yet the very system that issued those warnings forced us into schedules that guaranteed exhaustion. The "solutions" they offered—nap in an on-call room, tell someone you're too tired, call an Uber—were flimsy Band-Aids on a wound that kept bleeding.

I am ashamed to admit how often I drove in that state. On the worst mornings, I even caught myself thinking that a car accident might solve the problem for me. Not because I wanted to hurt anyone else— never that—but because an injury felt like the only excuse the system would accept. Can you imagine hating your job so much that you'd risk your own life, just to be free of it for a while?

When I inevitably made it to work my body betrayed me in other ways. I moved like I was underwater, rereading orders I had just typed, staring at the cursor as if it might finish the note for me. My fingers dragged across the keyboard at a snail's pace. Time itself seemed to stretch, cruel and endless. When nurses gave me puzzled looks after I asked them to repeat a simple question on rounds, shame burned hot in my chest. My brain was fogged, and no amount of willpower could clear it.

If sleep was the match that lit the fire, energy was the fuel it consumed.

Energy: I didn't have any. This symptom goes hand in hand with sleep. It's obvious—when you aren't sleeping, you aren't going to have energy. But it went beyond fatigue into marrow-deep depletion, the sense that every ounce of strength had been wrung out of me and there was nothing left to give. Even on weekends, when I could sleep late, I still could not summon the willpower to get out of bed. At the time, I hated myself for it. Looking back, I realize it wasn't laziness—it was illness.

One night in particular stands out to me. After a string of overstimulating ER shifts, I walked out the sliding doors into the parking garage, the fluorescent lights buzzing overhead, and collapsed into the driver's seat of my car. I didn't even turn the key. For fifteen minutes, I just sat there gripping the steering wheel, staring at nothing. The silence was intoxicating. No alarms, no shouting patients, no overhead pages, just stillness.

That silence should have been a relief, but it also revealed how empty I was. Lifting my hand to start the ignition felt like too much. Eventually I drove home, but even that felt dangerous—as if I was driving on autopilot. When I walked through the door, Tyler asked how my shift went, and I couldn't answer. I just shook my head, too drained for words. Tears welled in my eyes, something that had become routine. Tyler reached in to hug me to try to make it better. I couldn't even summon the energy to hug him back.

That was the cruelest part of all: not only did I have nothing left for myself, I also had nothing left for the person I loved most.

And when your energy is gone, food quickly follows.

Appetite: I lost weight during my depression. As a woman in the twenty-first century, I have a complicated relationship with weight. Despite knowing objectively that the loss wasn't good, I was secretly

31

pleased to see my clothes fit more loosely. People at work noticed, and it was hard not to bask in that praise. Even so, I was deliberate about intake. Despite not wanting to eat, I forced myself to drink high-calorie shakes and reached for easy snacks to hit a daily minimum.

The lack of appetite was strange—I've always loved food, especially dessert. My sweet tooth virtually disappeared. On my twenty-seventh birthday (a day I cried three separate times), Tyler took me to an Italian restaurant I loved. I didn't finish my pasta and, when we ordered dessert, I got the chocolate gelato out of obligation. I didn't even want it. My past and current self would balk at this. Not wanting gelato? An abomination. That's what depression does. It alters your basic human drives.

Even on ordinary days, food became a chore. Tyler would cook dinner—something simple and comforting like tacos or stir-fry—and I would sit at the table, staring at the plate as if it were another task I had to get through. I'd take a few bites, chew mechanically, then push the food around to make it look like I'd eaten more than I had. In the hospital cafeteria, I gravitated toward "safe foods": a bagel, a banana, maybe a granola bar. Bland, easy to swallow, requiring no decisions. I avoided the hot food line altogether. The thought of picking out a full tray—of making choices—was too much.

The strangest part was watching this happen from the inside. I knew the Diagnostic and Statistical Manual of Mental Disorders (DSM) criteria. I knew loss of appetite was a symptom. But it was surreal to feel my own body rebelling against something so basic. Depression didn't just take away hunger; it stole the rituals I associated with joy—trying a new recipe, splitting dessert with Tyler, lingering over a meal with friends. Eating became purely functional, a box to check so my body could keep going another day.

And as appetite disappeared, movement slowed to a crawl.

Psychomotor: this one's less familiar to those outside psychiatry. It comes in two flavors: psychomotor agitation or retardation. I had the latter, which showed itself as lack of desire to do literally anything. On my days off, I stayed in bed for hours. I couldn't even bring myself to walk the dog.

Ralphie would wait by the door with his leash, tail wagging, ready for the one thing in his day that brought him joy. I would look at him and feel a pang of guilt so sharp it made me nauseous. I wanted to move, to reach for the leash, to open the door—but my body wouldn't cooperate. It was as if a layer of lead weighed down my arms and legs. Eventually Tyler would come home from work and take Ralphie out himself. I'd roll over in bed, ashamed, sometimes pretending to be asleep because that was less humiliating than being awake and near-catatonic.

That same heaviness crept into every corner of my life. Folding laundry felt like climbing a mountain. Sending a simple text back to a friend required more activation energy than studying for Step exams ever had. Even the smallest motions were delayed, as if I were wading through molasses. Tyler picked up the slack—cooking, cleaning, walking the dog, even initiating conversations when all I could do was sit silently on the couch. Depression didn't just slow me down; it shifted the balance of our marriage, pushing him into caretaker mode when all either of us wanted was a partner.

Psychomotor agitation, on the other hand, is more common in elderly patients or those with melancholic depression. It presents as pacing, hand-wringing, inability to sit still, restlessness. I didn't have this, so I can't speak to it personally, but it sounds immensely uncomfortable. For me, the opposite was true: stillness wasn't uncomfortable. It was the only thing I could manage.

Conclusion: With sleep and appetite, some people swing the other way: sleeping excessively or eating constantly. As for appetite, I'm somewhat grateful mine diminished. Thanks to a society where a size six model was once considered "plus-sized," I had complicated feelings about weight loss. I knew it wasn't healthy, but the praise still felt good. That's the messed-up thing about living in a culture obsessed with thinness.

Depression is often thought of as a disease of the mind, but my experience showed me how powerfully it manifests in the body. While I could hide the racing thoughts and self-doubt, the physical changes betrayed me: weight falling off, movements slowing, reluctance to join colleagues for even a short walk around the hospital. Those outward signs were impossible to mask, and in some ways, they spoke louder than anything I felt inside. That is one of the cruelest aspects of depression—it alters the most basic human drives, and even when you try to keep it private, your body tells the story.

Sleep, energy, appetite, movement—all of them twisted into versions of themselves that no longer resembled me. Depression took what was automatic and made it effortful. It stole what was joyful and made it hollow.

Depression comes in many flavors, and what I've described here is just my own. In the coming chapters, I'll share the stories of patients whose depression looked very different, proof that this illness wears many faces, and none of them should be ignored.

CHAPTER FIVE
When the Healer Needs Healing

There is an unbelievable stigma within the medical profession regarding seeking help for your mental health. In the last chapter, I revealed the origin of my depression: the lack of sleep and imposter syndrome instilled in me during my emergency medicine rotation. I was fortunate that there was a third-year resident who took me under her wing in that hectic, sometimes terrifying, ER. I'll call her Monica.

She saved my life.

On my third day in the ER, after a horrific night of sleep, I showed up to work and immediately knew I needed to get help. I was hyperventilating—I had called my mom and cried on the way to work—and I could feel my heart beating out of my chest. I was silent, I didn't even say hi to my coworkers. I was more than anxious; I was unraveling from the inside out. I didn't know where to turn, but I found Monica and she helped me, for which I am eternally grateful.

Monica told me about the employee assistance program (EAP), which I touched on briefly in an earlier chapter. It provided mental health support for hospital employees and was entirely anonymous and confidential, an important tenet of psychiatric care. Monica gave me the phone number, and I stepped outside and immediately called. I spoke to an on-call mental health counselor who helped me realize that I was, in fact, not dying and that everything would probably be okay. I spoke to that counselor for over an hour and returned to the ER feeling marginally more in control of my emotions. I was still mentally and physically exhausted, but slightly less scared of the ER.

Here's the thing: I was so scared to even admit to Monica that I needed help. Despite knowing all the common symptoms and warning signs, it's hard for doctors to recognize within themselves when something is wrong, and even harder to verbalize that feeling and share it with a colleague. I turned to Monica in my time of need because there was no one else in that hospital I could go to. I had zero friends, very few trusted superiors (attending physicians whom I had worked with before), and no leadership that seemed approachable. I was at my wit's end; I was *this* close to leaving work without permission and driving myself to the nearest urgent care to get some sort of anxiety medicine.

It was that bad.

I'm proud of myself for how I handled that day—and the remainder of my ER rotation—because I proved that I am a capable physician. I may not have enjoyed the unexpected nature and pace of working in emergency medicine, but I knew what I was doing. I just had to slow myself down and breathe before deciding how to manage a patient. I could have left. I'm sure my supervisors would have understood— even doctors need sick days. Or, maybe, a mental health day?

However, *many* doctors would frown upon the concept of a mental health day. There is a massive stigma associated with experiencing mental health struggles. Some associate it with weakness, an underlying inferiority within the psyche. I think what scares people most is that if a doctor admits to struggling mentally, it calls everything into question—their judgment, their competence, their right to be in the room. But the truth is, struggling doesn't make you less of a doctor. If anything, it makes you more human. And medicine could use a little more of that.

I didn't fix everything in a day, of course. But that call to EAP was the first time I let myself say out loud: I'm not okay. It was the first small crack in the wall I had built around myself—the one labeled "strong doctor who can handle anything." The counselor on the other end of the phone helped me name what I was experiencing: burnout, anxiety, depression. We didn't solve it all in that hour, but I felt lighter walking back into the ER than I had in weeks. Just being heard, without judgment, was medicine.

In the days that followed, I scheduled more sessions through EAP and made an appointment with my primary care physician (PCP). That's when I restarted Lexapro. I remember picking up the prescription and feeling a complicated mix of shame and hope. Shame, because I had internalized the idea that needing help meant I had failed. Hope, because maybe I didn't have to feel like this forever.

This is the part I wish more people in medicine talked about: how deeply damaging the culture of silence is. We're trained to ignore our own pain, to show up no matter what, to never let our vulnerabilities interfere with patient care. But what about when they already are? What about when we're drowning and no one notices because we've all been taught to swim silently?

I want to believe that our generation of doctors is changing that. We talk more. We go to therapy. We check on each other. The truth is, even healers need healing—and I refuse to be ashamed of that ever again.

Before moving on, I want to pause and consider what might have happened that day if I hadn't had Monica to turn to.

I likely would never have found out about EAP—those six, free phone therapy sessions, which helped me immensely. I probably would have left work that day. I was running on fumes, inches away from a full-blown panic attack, and desperate for the safety of a dark, quiet room where I could finally breathe.

Without saying out loud, to a stranger on the other end of the line, that I was depressed, I might not have made the next decision: calling my PCP and restarting Lexapro. As simple as it sounds, that SSRI was a turning point in my mental health.

So, thank you, Monica. For noticing. For listening. For being the person I could go to when I didn't know where else to turn.

Because that was the day the healer needed healing—and finally, she got it.

CHAPTER SIX
The Quietly Cruel Culture of Medicine

In the last chapter, I hinted at the brutality of medicine. Some people in this field are so intelligent, so razor-sharp, that their competence turns into a weapon. It's not the kind of weapon you can see—there's no scalpel or syringe in their hand—but a subtler, sharper one: words, tone, and the quiet implication that you are less. Less worthy of your position. Less valuable in your white coat. Less deserving of being in the room at all.

This is the darker side of medicine and medical education, the part that makes me sometimes wish I'd chosen something else. Not because I don't love the work. I do. I love my patients, the intellectual challenge, the privilege of being trusted with someone's mind and body. But the culture? That's another story.

I believe my generation of physicians can, and will, change that culture. I see it already in the way we check in on each other, the way we talk openly about mental health, the way we question "the way it's always been done." But before we can get to that better future, I have to tell you about the present.

The cruelty I'm talking about isn't always the kind that's shouted in your face. Sometimes it's the kind that never even looks up. The kind that doesn't remember your name. That answers your question with a smirk instead of words. That lets the silence stretch so long you start to wish you'd never spoken at all.

There was a moment during intern year that I think about more often than I'd like. It wasn't the most traumatic thing that ever happened to me in medicine, not even close, but it lodged itself in my brain like a splinter. An irritating memory I wish I could get rid of.

It happened during my ICU month, one of the most formative rotations of my training. That month truly built me up as a physician, but it also showed me exactly how medicine can grind people down. I had an attending that everyone feared. Not respected—feared. He could walk onto the unit and the air would change. Shoulders would tense. Eyes would drop to the floor. Conversations would cut off mid-sentence.

We'll call him "Dr. Mather." Before I ever worked with him, I knew his reputation: intense, brilliant, uncompromising. What I didn't know was that the particular brand of intensity he specialized in was one that relied on public humiliation as a teaching method.

Dr. Mather loved to "pimp" his learners. In medicine, that word means to fire off rapid, often obscure medical questions to students and residents, usually in the middle of rounds. It's supposed to be a teaching tool. In reality, it feels like a verbal firing squad. Get the answer wrong, and the moment turns into a performance—not for the patient, but for the rest of the team—of just how little you know.

One morning, we were rounding outside a critically ill patient's room. He zeroed in on a third-year medical student—someone still brand new to the hospital floors—and asked for the detailed mechanism of action of levetiracetam (Keppra). When the student hesitated, he barked, "You don't know? You're telling me you're in your third year of medical school and you don't know this?" His voice was loud enough to turn heads at the nurses' station.

Here's the thing: that's not something most medical students would know. It's not even something most interns would know unless they'd rotated through neurology. And yet, in that moment, it wasn't about knowledge. It was about dominance.

By some stroke of luck, I never found myself on the receiving end of Dr. Mather's wrath. This was not because I was some kind of prodigy—I'm not. I passed the exams, I do my job, but I could not, even today, recite the exact mechanism of Keppra from memory. I got lucky. For reasons I still don't understand, he spared me. But he didn't spare anyone else.

And here's the part that's hardest to admit: I didn't speak up. Not once. Not when he dressed down a medical student until her eyes filled with tears. Not when he mocked a resident for needing to look up a lab value. Not when he delivered one of his monologues about our collective incompetence, a lecture he seemed to enjoy giving as much as other people enjoy telling a good joke.

The shame of my silence is something I carry. But I also know—and anyone who's been in that position will know—that speaking up would have been professional suicide. The ICU runs on a strict hierarchy. The attending is at the top of the food chain, the final authority on every decision. Beneath them are the fellows and senior residents, then the interns, and finally, the medical students. I was near the very bottom, with the only rung below me occupied by those students. If I had stood up for them, I'd have become the next target.

And the truth? No one would've backed me. Not even the people I was defending. Not because they agreed with him—they didn't—but because they were trying to survive too. In that room, survival meant silence. That's what I mean by the *quiet* cruelty of medicine. Not just the cutting remarks, the public call-outs, the way someone can make you feel small with a single question. But the silence of everyone around them. The silence that says: this is fine. This is normal. This is how it's done.

I still think about those rounds. I still picture the way no one met each other's eyes after he walked away. How the medical student he'd humiliated stood a little apart from the group, shoulders hunched, looking very small in her short white coat. How I wanted to go to her, to say something, but didn't. I told myself I'd do it later.

I never did.

Maybe one day I'll be in a position to break that silence without risking my own career. Maybe I already am, and I need to find the courage. But at the time, I was just trying to get through each day without becoming someone else's object lesson. And in medicine, especially in the ICU, that's sometimes all survival means.

Dr. Mather's brand of cruelty was obvious—loud, theatrical, impossible to miss. But the truth is, most of the cruelty in medicine doesn't shout. It whispers. It hides in the pauses, the glances, the way people choose not to speak to you. And once I started noticing it, I realized it was everywhere.

I noticed it in the way a senior resident seemed to forget I existed. On my second rotation, in nephrology, I barely saw the third-year resident assigned to work with me. I emailed her at the start of the month to introduce myself, and I kid you not, I saw her maybe twice in the next four weeks. She didn't check in, didn't teach, didn't even ask how things were going. She wasn't cruel in the traditional sense—she simply didn't care. My presence or absence made no difference to her, and my learning was nowhere on her radar.

I noticed it in the dreaded, dismissive response: *Look it up.* More often than not, when I asked an attending a question about a patient's treatment plan, that answer was all I got. No discussion, no context, just the verbal equivalent of a closed door. Maybe there's some hidden brilliance in this form of medical teaching, but to me it feels like a cop-out. Yes, self-directed learning is valuable. But it's not the same as being taught. And when you're working twelve-hour days managing someone else's patients, it's hard not to feel that the least they could do is take five minutes to explain something to you.

I noticed it during my ER month—the one where I worked with Monica, the angel I told you about in the last chapter. But even Monica's warmth couldn't cancel out the chill from multiple attendings who never learned my name. Day after day, I walked into the ER, and day after day, I was met with the same blank, searching looks. There's nothing quite like realizing that if you walked out mid-shift, no one would notice. I wondered if I should have walked out that day I had a panic attack.

I noticed it in the way I was excluded without anyone saying the words. As a transitional year resident, I knew my time at that hospital was temporary. Our class didn't go out of its way to make friends— maybe because we knew we'd be gone in twelve months. But the categorical residents, the ones who'd be there for three years, didn't make much effort either. There were mornings I'd arrive for sign-out to find the whole team laughing about the boat day they'd shared over the weekend. I hadn't been invited. No one even pretended to have forgotten. Being left out, again and again, might sound small—but repeated enough times, it becomes its own kind of cruelty. The quiet kind. The kind you feel in your chest, not your ears.

CHAPTER SEVEN
Gaslighting Myself into Functioning

When you're dragging yourself into the hospital and the only thing keeping you upright is the two hundred milligrams of caffeine sloshing through your veins, and you start calling that "functioning," you're lying to yourself. Burnout has been rebranded as a badge of honor, but it's really just a slow form of self-destruction. Somewhere along the way, we decided it was normal for residents to live on the brink—not of greatness, but of collapse. I told myself this was fine. I told myself I could handle it. I gaslit myself into believing survival was the same thing as living.

I'd pull into work—thoroughly caffeinated but still hollowed-out under the surface—and let the mask slide into place. Smile at my co-residents. Swipe my badge into the workroom. Boot up the archaic electronic medical record system. Print my patient list. Make small talk about weekends, because the system convinced us that's when life was allowed to happen.

Then I'd start pre-rounding: eight patients to see, three to four minutes each, just enough time to check boxes before moving on. The unspoken rule from insurance was simple:—if you weren't doing something for them today, they didn't belong in a hospital bed. I'd paste on my smile before walking into each room. These patients were sick; the last thing they needed was a doctor who looked as depleted as they felt.

By the time I'd seen everyone twice, once for pre-rounding, once for "real" rounds, a fierce headache would be blooming behind my eyes. I'd retreat to the resident workroom to hammer out notes, my vision going grainy at the edges, until the pager shrieked with two new admissions from the ER.

If you do what I just described enough days in a row, the facade starts to crack. And once the shell breaks, the yolk doesn't stay neatly contained—it spills, messy and impossible to ignore.

That's what happened one morning in a hospital stairwell, a few weeks into my three-month stint on internal medicine. I was already fraying when, during rounds, my attending casually mentioned how much he looked forward to his week off—attendings worked seven days on, seven days off. The math hit me like a gut punch: four more years before I might have that kind of breathing room. Over a thousand more days of residency, and I felt like I couldn't get through one.

I mumbled something about needing the bathroom and slipped away, tears already welling. The stairwell was cramped and airless, the kind of still heat that makes panic bloom faster. My chest tightened. I reached for my phone, thumb hovering over Tyler's name before I remembered he had a big day at work.

Disturbing him felt selfish.

Plan B: distraction. A five-minute doomscroll, the Gen Z version of a deep breath. I sat on the hard concrete step, letting TikTok fill my vision: dancing videos, absurd comedy sketches, and the latest trending outrage—each one pulling me a millimeter further from myself. It worked, in its strange way. When I stood up, the tears had receded, the panic dulled. I rejoined the team, smile in place, ready to make it through the rest of the day.

It didn't stop there. Once my shell had cracked, the fissures just kept spreading.

One night, after a brutal day at the hospital, I walked in, dropped my bag, and sank straight to the living room floor, —still in my scrubs and shoes. The carpet prickled through the thin fabric of my pants, gritty with dog hair and crumbs. I rolled my eyes, wishing Tyler had vacuumed over the weekend so I wouldn't be lying in it.

I immediately hated myself for the thought. He worked almost as much as I did, with a commute twice as long. A dirty rug wasn't his fault. Still, the irritation clung to me.

Fifteen minutes into my self-appointed floor time keys jingled in the lock. I sat up, numb, as he walked in, peeled off his shoes and socks, and,—without thinking,—tossed the socks on the floor by the dining table. It was as if the socks left his hand in slow motion and something in me snapped.

"God, do you have to be such a slob?" I blurted.

His head jerked up, surprise flashing across his face. I instantly regretted it, but instead of backing off, I doubled down: "How hard is it to just walk upstairs and take your socks off there? Put them in the laundry basket. It's not rocket science."

He stared at me as if he didn't recognize the person in front of him.

42

This was his routine. He'd always taken his socks off when he got home (don't ask me why; I can't explain the whims of a man), and it never once bothered me before that night.

In silence, he scooped up the socks and carried them upstairs, leaving me alone with my shame.

It was just a pair of socks. But in that moment, it felt like the whole damn rug was unraveling under me.

A few days later, another crack.

It was late morning, rounds almost done, my now-routine headache starting to bloom behind my eyes when it happened. My attending—one I actually liked—asked for our leukemia patient's hemoglobin level. I should have known. But I didn't.

It wasn't on my list, and it clearly hadn't stuck in my head. I rifled through my papers anyway, pretending to search, but I was just buying time. Finally, I looked up and admitted I didn't know. The attending waved it off,——but my senior's eyes had gone hard, his lips pressed into a line.

We wrapped up rounds and headed toward the cafeteria. As I followed the med student to the elevators, my senior caught my arm, holding me back. His grip was firm but not painful,—just enough to keep me in place.

"You need to get here earlier and have every pertinent lab written down," he said evenly. "Mistakes like that might seem negligible, but they add up. They make you look like a careless intern. Step it up if you want to prove yourself to Dr. G."

Each sentence landed like a small bullet. My face flushed hot. I nodded, excused myself to the bathroom, and shut the door behind me. Cool water over my face. Deep breaths. A whispered, "you've got this," to my flustered reflection in the mirror.

When I came out, he was waiting to walk to lunch together—a strange, almost tender gesture after the reprimand. But even that small kindness didn't stop the crack from widening.

The cracks in my little-miss-perfect intern act were widening, and it was clear my colleagues noticed. No one said anything. Honestly, I think they just didn't have the emotional bandwidth to extend themselves—residency was hard for everyone, not just me.

This was the reality of my world during those dark days: I had a version of myself who was clad in scrubs and a white coat, and another version who existed only within the confines of my home or alone in my car. "Doctor Me" smiled at patients, nodded dutifully at seniors, and documented every lab value in the chart. On the surface, she looked competent, maybe even steady. But the real me was sobbing in stairwells and silently begging for a day off that would never come. I felt like an actor in my own life, delivering lines I didn't believe, terrified someone would catch me breaking character. The worst part was how convincing I'd become—how easily people believed in Doctor Me while the real me was dissolving behind the curtain.

With no friends or mentors to lean on, I finally shattered at home. After a brutal shift with two complex admissions—a severe heart failure patient on a dozen meds and a young girl with a rare autoimmune disease I'd never treated—I drove home in silence, my usual decompression ritual.

But I never fully decompressed. When I walked in, Ralphie greeted me with his usual unbridled enthusiasm, and I cried. Not a tear or two—a full, heaving sob. I hadn't cried like that since the Match Day email nearly a year before, and this was the third time in as many days.

I dropped my bag and lunchbox, ripped my stethoscope from my neck so fast it yanked my hair, and sat on the floor. Ralphie licked at my tears, tail still wagging. I grabbed my phone and FaceTimed Arielle, my best friend.

The ringtone mixed with my sobs, creating a strange dissonance. She picked up on the third ring, took one look, and just stayed with me while I cried. Ari had been through her own brutal months of residency—she didn't need me to explain. She stayed on the line while I dragged myself upstairs, brushed my teeth through tears, and tried to convince myself sleep might make it better.

But every time I felt a flicker of okay, the dread came back. Nine more weeks of internal medicine. It was like a tunnel with no light at the end.

This was the closest I'd come to being suicidal. Ari, with her family medicine training, asked if I felt safe. I told her yes, even though I wasn't sure. Tyler would be home soon; he'd make sure I was okay. She watched me take a melatonin. We both hoped it would work.

I didn't want to kill myself, not exactly. But I did hope for something tragic and painless in my sleep. A ruptured aneurysm. Gone in seconds. No suffering.

PART TWO

SURVIVING

This part is about endurance. Faking it 'til you make it, putting on a mask, showing up when you're barely standing. These songs hold the weight of intern year, but also the first flickers of hope—therapy calls, Lexapro, the reminder that maybe you can keep going.

CHAPTER EIGHT
Swing Shift

If intern year was a marathon, the month I spent on swing shift was where my legs first started to buckle. It wasn't technically "night float" and it wasn't technically "day team," but some warped hybrid of the two: five p.m. to midnight, every day for a month. In theory, that kind of schedule was supposed to be easier on our bodies than true nights. In reality, it chewed me up and spat me out.

The hospital never sleeps, but the rhythms change as the day fades. On swing shift, I lived in the liminal space between the orderly chaos of days and the eerie stillness of nights. The dayshift residents would be hustling to wrap things up, tying off loose ends, signing out patients, eager to get home for dinner. And just as they exhaled, I would be walking in, badge clipped on, stethoscope slung around my neck, already bracing for the handoff list of everything that was "pending."

The handoffs themselves were demoralizing. *This patient is stable, just follow up their potassium. This one's pending a CT scan, can you chase down the result? This guy might decompensate, keep an eye on him.* In other words: we did the big stuff, now you babysit. By the time I logged in, the cafeteria was closing, the hallways were emptying, and I was just getting started.

What made that month brutal wasn't just the work, it was the timing. Five p.m. to midnight meant missing dinner with Tyler every single night. It's amazing how much not sharing a meal can hurt. Dinner had been our anchor, the one time we reliably sat across from each other, even if the day had been chaotic. Losing it meant losing him, in a way.

I tried to pretend it was no big deal. "We'll do brunch on the weekends," I said brightly, as though an eggs Benedict on Saturday could replace thirty consecutive missed dinners. But the truth is, I missed him desperately. I would come home around twelve-thirty or one in the morning, and the house would be dark. Sometimes he left a plate of food covered with foil, which I'd eat standing at the counter, cold forkfuls of pasta or congealed stir-fry. More often I was too wired to eat. The adrenaline of the hospital clung to me, buzzing in my veins. My stomach churned, my appetite gone. I'd crawl into bed next to him, but he was already asleep, turned away, breathing deeply.

There's something uniquely isolating about sliding under the sheets beside the person you love most and realizing you're living parallel lives. We were in the same house, even the same bed, but I felt like we were missing each other by miles.

Everyone warned me that swing shifts messed with sleep. I thought I'd be fine. After all, I had survived college all-nighters, marathon study sessions in med school, even a few nights of true night float already.

But this was different.

Midnight is late, but it's not late enough. By the time I drove home, showered, and tried to unwind, it was two in the morning at best. Yet my body didn't treat it like a true night shift; I couldn't sleep until four, sometimes five. And no matter what time I fell asleep, my eyes would snap open at nine a.m., uselessly alert.

That meant four or five hours of broken, jittery rest per day. Not enough to recover. Not enough to reset. Certainly not enough to stay sane.

Sleep deprivation does strange things. It makes the world blur at the edges, like someone turned the contrast down on reality. It made me irritable with nurses, sharp with medical students, and less patient with those I was caring for. I hated myself for that. I had entered medicine determined to never become the bitter, brusque residents I'd encountered as a student. But there I was, halfway through swing month, rolling my eyes at a midnight page for chest pain and muttering, "Of course he has chest pain, he's in the hospital."

That wasn't me. Or at least, it wasn't the me I wanted to be. But sleep deprivation erodes identity. It scrapes you raw until all that's left is survival instinct.

What made swing shifts worse than nights was the sense of being untethered. On true nights, at least you suffer with a team. There's a camaraderie in seeing the same bleary-eyed faces every dusk, trading jokes at two a.m., sharing vending machine snacks like they're gourmet meals. Swing shift was different. The day team didn't want me—they were winding down. The night team didn't know me—I was leaving as they arrived. I floated in the in-between, part of nothing. There was only one resident at a time working the swing shift, which was isolating in itself.

It mirrored how I felt in life. Too awake to be with Tyler, too exhausted to be with friends, too "off" to do anything but drag myself through the motions. I stopped texting people back. I stopped making weekend plans. I stopped reading, which for me was the clearest sign something was wrong. The very things that had sustained me in med school—books, friendships, family—fell away.

All I did was swing shift, stumble home, fail to sleep, and repeat.

My body betrayed me that month. The headaches came first, pounding temples that no amount of ibuprofen could dull. Then the GI issues—nausea, heartburn, stomach cramps. My appetite disappeared. I dropped a few pounds, and people commented on how "great" I looked. I smiled thinly, but inside I wanted to scream: this isn't health, it's collapse.

There were moments I caught myself fantasizing about illness. Nothing catastrophic—just something bad enough to get me admitted, tucked into a hospital bed where no one could page me. That's how far I'd fallen: the idea of being a patient sounded like relief.

Looking back, I can see it clearly: swing shift was the beginning of the end. The month that set the stage for my breakdown. At the time, I couldn't name it. I thought I was just "tired." Just "adjusting." But now I know: isolation plus sleep deprivation plus relentless work is a formula for collapse.

One night near the end of rotation, I was sitting in the resident lounge at 11:45 p.m., waiting for the clock to tick down to midnight. I had finished my sign-outs, my patients were tucked in, and there was nothing left to do. The halls were quiet, the overhead lights buzzing faintly. My phone was silent, my inbox empty. And yet I couldn't make myself leave. I sat there staring at the linoleum floor, paralyzed. Going home meant facing the darkness of my quiet house, the silence of Tyler's even breaths beside me, the certainty that I would lie awake for hours.

I remember thinking: *I am so alone.* The thought didn't come with tears, just a dull ache in my chest.

What did I learn from that month? That survival isn't always about catastrophe. Sometimes it's about the slow grind, the steady erosion, the daily absence of joy. Swing shift taught me that isolation can be as dangerous as any code blue, and that missing dinner with the person you love can cut deeper than missing a lab value.

It taught me that medicine doesn't just take your time; it warps it. It rearranges your circadian rhythm, your family rhythm, your life rhythm, until you hardly recognize yourself.

And it taught me that my breaking point wasn't sudden. It was cumulative. It started here, in the fluorescent glow of a half-empty hospital, during a month when I was neither day nor night, neither here nor there.

I survived swing shift. I showed up every night at five p.m., stayed until midnight, and dragged myself home. I answered the pages, wrote the notes, followed up on the potassium, chased the CT results. On paper, I did my job.

But surviving isn't the same as living. Swing shift hollowed me out, made me a ghost in my own life. It stole dinners with my husband, it stole rest, it stole joy. It made me feel like a visitor in my own house, a stranger in my own skin.

When people ask me about the worst month of intern year, they expect me to say ICU, wards, or call nights. But the truth is, it was swing shift—the month that didn't look hard on the schedule but nearly broke me anyway.

Because survival isn't only about what happens in the hospital. It's about what happens when you walk out those doors. And that month, I wasn't surviving at all. I was dissolving.

CHAPTER NINE
Meds, Therapy, Hope

By the time I finally started Lexapro during intern year, I was
drowning. Three months of back-to-back inpatient medicine had
stripped me bare, and I had nothing left to give—not to my patients,
not to my husband, not to myself. I'd taken SSRIs before, but this time
was different; this time, it felt like a lifeline. Therapy came next,
courtesy of the hospital's EAP—six phone calls with a stranger who,
for the first time in months, made me feel seen. And then, quietly, the
calendar kept turning. Medicine ended, psychiatry began, and
somewhere along the way, the darkness started to loosen its grip. The
combination of medication, therapy, and the slow but relentless
passage of time didn't just make me feel better, it gave me back a
reason to believe I could thrive.

Lexapro didn't fix everything overnight. In fact, the first two weeks
were the hardest. I swallowed each pill with a mix of desperation and
doubt, clinging to the promise that one day I might wake up and not
feel so unbearably heavy. I had taken SSRIs before—in high school and
college—but back then I was almost casual about them, like they were
just part of the background of growing up anxious. This time was
different. This time I was an intern drowning in twelve-hour shifts,
admitting patient after patient while silently wondering if I wanted to
wake up for another day of it. This time, the medication felt less like a
crutch and more like a lifeline.

Therapy came next, and though it was just six phone calls with
someone I never met in person, it cracked something open in me. It's
strange how talking to a stranger can feel safer than talking to the
people you love. With my husband, I held back because I didn't want
to scare him. With my family, I minimized, afraid of disappointing
them. But with this anonymous voice on the other end of the line, I let
myself tell the truth: that I thought I'd made a mistake going into
medicine, that I fantasized about not waking up, that I didn't know

who I was outside of my white coat. And instead of recoiling, she listened. She didn't try to rush me into gratitude or insist that things "would get better." She simply acknowledged that what I was carrying was heavy, and that I didn't have to carry it alone.

Slowly, the edges softened. It wasn't dramatic—no lightning bolt, no miraculous morning where I felt like my old self again. It was more like the fog thinning. A day when I laughed at something my co-resident said in the workroom. An evening when I had the energy to cook instead of pouring cereal into a bowl. A morning when I caught myself looking forward to clinic. These small shifts strung together became something bigger: hope.

By the time I finally started to feel like myself again, I was a little embarrassed at how much I had resisted. Why had I waited so long? Why had I convinced myself that I should be able to do this without medication or therapy, as if white-knuckling my way through depression would somehow make me stronger? That's the lie so many of us in medicine believe—that suffering is noble, that asking for help is weakness. But I know better now. Taking Lexapro wasn't weakness. Calling the EAP wasn't weakness. Those choices saved my life.

It's a lesson I carry with me every time I prescribe medication to a patient. I see the hesitation in their eyes when I bring up an SSRI. *I don't want to be dependent on a pill. What if this changes me? What if it doesn't work?* I know those questions intimately, because I asked them too. And so instead of brushing past them with a rehearsed explanation of serotonin and neurotransmitters, I sit with them in the doubt. I tell them that taking medication isn't about changing who you are, it's about giving you the chance to see yourself clearly again.

I'll never forget one of my first outpatient patients: a young woman in her twenties, barely able to speak through tears. She told me she felt broken, useless, and hopeless. She said she couldn't imagine a future where she felt anything other than despair. As she sat in front of me, hair unwashed, eyes red-rimmed, I recognized myself in her. The way she spoke about dragging herself through each day was the same way I had narrated my own life to that anonymous therapist months earlier.

I started her on an SSRI. She looked at me skeptically, but she agreed to try. At her follow-up a month later, she was cautious but different. "I don't feel great," she admitted. "But I feel … less terrible. I showered yesterday. I called my sister. I don't know, I think maybe something is shifting."

I wanted to leap out of my chair and cheer for her. Because that was exactly how it had felt for me, too: not a magical fix, but a slight loosening of the weight, a small light creeping in at the edges. I told her what I tell all my patients now: that getting better is often about celebrating the smallest victories. Showering, cooking one meal, calling a loved one. They may not feel monumental, but they are proof that the fog can lift.

Six months later, she came back for a routine check-in. Her hair was freshly cut, and she told me she had enrolled in community college. "I don't think I would've had the energy to do this before," she said. "But now, it feels possible."

Possible.

That word still catches in my throat. Because for a long time, I couldn't imagine a future that felt possible either. But medication, therapy, and time changed that for me—and seeing it change someone else reminded me why I do this work.

Hope doesn't always arrive with fanfare. Sometimes it tiptoes in quietly, disguised as ordinary life: a hot shower, a phone call, a meal cooked in your own kitchen. Other times it comes in bigger waves, like getting married, starting residency in the specialty you love, or sitting down to write the book you once thought you'd never have the strength to finish.

I called this chapter *meds, therapy, hope* because for me, they are inseparable. The medication steadied me. The therapy gave me words for what I was feeling. And hope—fragile at first, then sturdier with time—became the thread that wove everything back together.

CHAPTER TEN
Finding Meaning in the ICU

By the time I landed in the ICU, I was running on fumes—physically, mentally, emotionally. Intern year had already wrung me dry, and yet here I was, stepping into a rotation that demanded more of me than any I'd done before. The ICU was not a place you coasted through; every patient was a high-wire act, every decision carried weight. I didn't have the luxury of checking out, even when I wanted to. Oddly, that was what kept me going. In a year where I often questioned why I was doing any of this at all, the ICU offered moments—fleeting, but undeniable—where my work felt meaningful. Sometimes, meaning is the only thing that keeps you alive in medicine.

Back in Chapter One, I touched on how meaningful my time there was, especially my experience with Pat, who sadly passed away after my shift one evening. Pat was not an isolated loss. During that month, I lost more patients than I could have ever prepared for. Until then, intern year had challenged me in countless ways, but I had never had a patient die under my care. That may seem improbable, but on the general wards most patients eventually left the hospital—often with more disability than they came in with, but still alive. The ICU was different. For Pat, and for many of my patients there, leaving with a beating heart was not part of the story.

Not every story had a sad ending—though very few had truly happy ones. Early in my rotation, I was called to a rapid response. In hospital terms, that's the alarm before the alarm: a patient is decompensating quickly, and a team rushes in to prevent a full code blue. This time, it was for a young woman I'll call "Destiny." She had cerebral palsy, which made her speech difficult to understand and gave her a body habitus that complicated her airway and lung function. She'd been admitted for pneumonia, and now she was struggling to breathe.

We quickly decided she needed to be transferred to the ICU, and as soon as she arrived, I presented her case to my attending. I ended with: "I think we'll need to intubate soon to give her the best shot." I didn't say the last two words out loud—at survival—but my attending heard them anyway. Destiny was deteriorating fast, and the decision had to be made. He told me to call her next of kin.

Her sister answered. She hesitated. She knew that in many cerebral palsy patients, intubation led not to recovery, but to a tracheostomy and permanent dependence on a ventilator—something she didn't want for Destiny. But she also knew the alternative: without intubation, Destiny might not live to see morning.

Consent was given. My attending told me to intubate. It was my first time, and my hands were shaking, but under his guidance the tube went in, and the ventilator took over. Destiny was still critically ill, but she was breathing, and she had a chance. In the ICU, sometimes that's the closest you get to a win.

Moments like that kept me going. They didn't erase the losses or make the ICU any less exhausting, but they reminded me why I was there. In a year when I often felt useless and out of place, those brief flashes of competence and purpose—helping someone live to see another sunrise—were enough to keep me moving forward.

The ICU rotation was notorious among my fellow interns as the hardest month of the year, but also one of the most rewarding. The intensity of caring for patients on the brink of death, the teamwork of leaning on nurses, respiratory therapists, and ICU pharmacists, the high stakes of knowing one small mistake could be fatal ... all of it cut through my intern-year disenchantment. It reminded me why I wanted to be a doctor in the first place: to make a difference.

The learning curve was steep, but by the end, I had never felt more competent, trusted, or useful than I did during those weeks caring for the sickest patients in the hospital. And in a year that often felt like an exercise in endurance, those moments of meaning were the lifelines that kept me from going under.

But here's what I didn't appreciate at the time: surviving in the ICU also meant learning how to carry the weight of so much death without collapsing under it. Until then, death had felt like a rare occurrence, something you read about in case studies or heard about secondhand. In the ICU, it was woven into daily life.

I began to notice how the team carried themselves after a patient died. Some of the seasoned nurses would pause at the bedside for a moment, resting a hand on the patient's arm before moving on to the next task. Respiratory therapists would stand in the hallway, quiet, their eyes distant, before returning to charting ventilator settings. The attendings rarely lingered; they moved briskly on to the next patient, as though momentum itself was a shield. They had been working alongside death for years and their skin was thick. I tried to follow their lead, but the grief had nowhere to go. More than once I found myself crying in the on-call room bathroom, muffling the sound with scratchy paper towels.

It was during those moments that I realized survival wasn't just physical, it was emotional. You had to metabolize grief fast enough to keep functioning, but slowly enough to avoid becoming numb.

That balance is harder than any medical decision I ever made.

The ICU also taught me the brutal paradox of critical care: you can be the most skilled physician in the world, and sometimes it still isn't enough. Machines can breathe for a patient, medications can squeeze every last drop of blood pressure from their veins, but at the end of the day, biology often wins.

I remember adjusting the orders for a norepinephrine drip on a man whose blood pressure kept plummeting despite maximum doses. I stared at the monitor, willing the numbers to climb, as if determination alone could raise a mean arterial pressure.

It didn't.

Within hours, his family was at the bedside, weeping as we withdrew support. I went home that night and stared at the ceiling, wondering if I had failed him, or if this was simply what it meant to practice medicine at the edge of life.

Teamwork was the lifeline of the ICU. The nurses were encyclopedias of practical wisdom: which patient was teetering on the brink, which IV line was about to fail, which family member needed additional information or support before they unraveled. I learned more from those bedside conversations than from any textbook. The respiratory therapists carried a quiet authority; when they told me a patient's lungs weren't tolerating a certain setting, I listened. The pharmacists caught interactions I hadn't even considered; they double-checked every order and saved many of my patients. By the end of the month, I realized medicine isn't practiced alone—it's an orchestra, and as an intern, I was lucky just to be in the ensemble.

There were lighter moments, too, though they were rare. On a long shift, after a successful code where a patient actually regained a pulse, one of the nurses high-fived me in the hallway. It was a small thing, but the warmth of it carried me for days. Another time, a family brought in homemade empanadas as a thank-you. We crowded into the break room, eating with gloved hands and exhaustion in our eyes, but for fifteen minutes, it felt like a celebration. Even in a place defined by suffering, joy found a way to sneak in through the cracks.

By the end of the rotation, I had grown in ways I didn't anticipate. I was no longer the tentative intern who second-guessed every order. I had placed central lines, titrated pressors, written death notes, and celebrated tiny victories. I'd intubated a young woman named Destiny, and I had stood with families as they made the hardest decisions of their lives. I learned that competence doesn't mean omnipotence, and that sometimes the most meaningful act is not saving a life but honoring a death.

Most of all, I realized that surviving as a doctor means collecting these moments—of loss, triumph, fear, humanity—and carrying them forward without letting them crush you. Surviving isn't stoicism. It isn't pretending the sadness isn't there. It's letting yourself feel it, then finding a way to return the next day and do it all again.

I don't know if I'll ever work in the ICU again. As a psychiatry resident, my days are filled with different kinds of crises—quieter, often invisible, but no less life-threatening. And yet, the lessons of that month follow me everywhere. They remind me that patients deserve honesty, families deserve compassion, and colleagues deserve kindness. They remind me that advance directives matter, that dignity matters, that sometimes letting go is as important as holding on.

Surviving that month didn't mean I walked away unscathed. It meant I walked away changed. It meant I found meaning in the chaos, if only in flashes. It meant I learned to trust myself, to lean on others, and to recognize that medicine is not about being invincible, it's about being present.

And maybe that's the secret no one tells you: in medicine, surviving isn't just about the patients. It's about us, too. It's about finding a way to keep going, even when the alarms are blaring, the losses are mounting, and the weight feels too heavy. It's about letting the rare moments of meaning—like Destiny's first breath on the ventilator, or a family's quiet gratitude—anchor you when everything else threatens to sweep you away.

Because at the end of the day, survival in medicine is not endurance for its own sake. It's endurance with purpose. And in the ICU, I found just enough of it to keep going.

CHAPTER ELEVEN
Friendship as a Lifeline

One of the hardest parts of intern year wasn't the hours, the patients, or even the relentless grind of call—it was the silence. After four years of medical school spent side by side with my best friends, studying for every exam together, suddenly we were scattered across the country.

I missed my girls.

It sucked. I went from having a built-in support system to spending nearly all my free time with only my husband and dog. Tyler loved me fiercely, but he couldn't carry the full weight of my sadness without it breaking him too. And as a transitional year resident, I never sought out real friendships with my co-residents.

That was a mistake.

I told myself I didn't need them, that this was just a pit stop before psychiatry, but the truth is, I needed people. I needed social support, and I wasn't getting it.

My medical school friends never disappeared. We texted daily, sometimes FaceTimed, and they did their best to buoy me through those long months. But they had something I didn't: belonging. They were in their "real" residency programs, forging new friendships, bonding with co-residents, and building a community. Meanwhile, I was suspended in a kind of limbo—part of the program but not really *in* it, physically present but emotionally absent.

Looking back, I can see that I underestimated how much of my happiness depended on other people. It's not that I didn't value my friendships—I knew how lucky I was to have them—but I thought daily texts could substitute for presence. They couldn't. In *The Anxious Generation*, Jonathan Haidt argues that online interaction is never a true replacement for face-to-face connection. He's right.

Talking over DMs or FaceTime isn't the same as laughing over coffee, venting during a walk, or collapsing into shared silence at the end of a long day. Intern year taught me this lesson the hard way:

humans need real social connection to survive, and no amount of scrolling or texting can fill that void.

Medical school and residency are different in countless ways, yet one is meant to prepare you for the other—a seamless handoff, a bridge from training wheels to the real thing.

That wasn't my experience.

I can't say for certain whether life would've felt easier had I matched into psychiatry the first time. But I know this: the leap from fourth-year medical student—with plenty of free time spent planning my wedding—to intern felt less like a transition and more like being hit by a stack of bricks.

The first few months of residency weren't all bad. I was still fresh, still glowing from the "I'm a doctor now" high, and still enjoying the newness of marriage at home. But fresh doesn't mean easy. The work itself was grueling. As a fourth-year medical student, even on your busiest internal medicine rotation, you might manage two or three patients at a time. As an intern, your list jumps to ten. Ten patients, each with multiple comorbidities, ten families waiting for updates, ten sets of labs and imaging studies to synthesize before rounds. It's not four times the responsibility—it felt like forty.

If residencies truly wanted to prepare medical students for what's ahead, they'd stop coddling them with artificially light workloads. Let them take five or six patients, not two. Let them feel the weight of the pager. Let them struggle with time management before the stakes are life-or-death. Because loving internal medicine when you're responsible for two patients isn't the same as surviving it when you're responsible for ten. With two, you can be thorough, you can dive into every detail of a patient's disease process, you can feel like an expert. With ten, you're forced to skate on the surface. You're just trying to keep your head above water long enough to discharge one patient before another gets admitted.

That whiplash, from being a student with time to breathe to being a doctor drowning in responsibility, was one of the most jarring parts of intern year. I enjoyed medical school. And now, in psychiatry, I genuinely enjoy residency. But intern year? Intern year was survival, plain and simple.

My friends felt the whiplash too. Arielle and Maha were thrown into the deep end of residency just like I was, but their experiences looked different. They were fully immersed in the specialties they'd chosen: family medicine for Arielle, physical medicine and rehabilitation for Maha. While I was stalled out on the side of the road in a transitional year, they were speeding down the highway at seventy-five miles per hour, gaining traction, building confidence, becoming the doctors they'd always hoped to be. This view may have been partly a warped vision of my mind pitting my situation against theirs, but it was grounded in reality: I had put my dream specialty on hold for a year of doing the kind of medicine I was least enchanted with.

I was so proud of them. Watching my best friends achieve their dreams was a gift. But pride and jealousy aren't mutually exclusive. I wanted what they had: a sense of forward motion, of being exactly where you're supposed to be. Instead, I felt suspended in limbo, my dream deferred.

Now that I've landed in psychiatry, that jealousy has evaporated. It's been replaced by something softer—joy, relief, gratitude. Seeing the three of us thrive in our own worlds makes me feel like we've all finally arrived. But back then, as an intern, I didn't feel like I was arriving anywhere. I was just hanging on, surviving day by day, waiting for the part of the story where my own life would start to feel like it was moving forward again.

Loneliness wasn't exclusive to friendship. I felt lonely in my marriage as well. This was no fault of Tyler's—he is truly the most loving and kind husband I could've dreamt up—but a fault of the system. I was working sixty-five to seventy-five hours a week, and he had a horrendous commute, regularly more than two hours round trip each day. Not only did we barely see each other, but when we finally did, we were both running on fumes. We'd collapse onto the couch or into bed, drained of any reserve energy that might have been spent on affection or nurturing our relationship. We weren't fighting, but we weren't really connecting either.

One Friday night stands out. We had planned a rare date night, something small but sacred: dinner at our favorite Italian place, maybe a walk downtown if we weren't too tired. I clung to the thought of it all week. Then, an accident on the highway doubled Tyler's commute. At almost the same moment, I got called about a late admission—a complicated heart failure patient who needed to be stabilized before I could leave. By the time I finished, the restaurant was closing. Tyler texted from his car that he was finally inching past the wreck, and we both admitted the obvious: it wasn't going to happen.

There was relief in the timing—at least neither of us was sitting alone at the table, waiting for the other. But the sadness was sharper. That was our one chance to connect that week, and it evaporated in a blur of brake lights and hospital alarms. I drove home in silence, and when I walked in, Tyler was already in sweats on the couch, half asleep with Ralphie curled beside him. We exchanged a tired smile, but that was it. No laughter, no lingering conversation over ravioli, no reminder that we were more than our jobs. Just two exhausted people missing each other even as we sat side by side.

Another facet of the loneliness we both struggled with during that first year of marriage, which happened to coincide with my intern year, was the abrupt loss of a social life. Weekly date nights went out the window. The cocktail-and-game nights we had loved hosting during medical school disappeared without warning. At the time, I thought those rituals were just "fun extras," nice little traditions but not essential. What I didn't realize until they were gone was how much they had buoyed us. Those evenings of laughter, clinking glasses, and friendly competition didn't just fill our social calendars—they filled our marriage with levity. They gave us common ground outside of medicine, commuting, and exhaustion. Without them, our life together felt stripped down to survival: two overworked people sharing a home, too tired to make it more than that.

There's a particular kind of ache that comes from lying next to the person you love most and still feeling lonely. It wasn't Tyler's fault, and it wasn't mine either. It was the structure of residency—the endless hours, the demands that spill over into every corner of your personal life—that created the distance. Medicine didn't just take me away from my friends; it stole the texture of my marriage, too.

Survival became the theme of that year—survival of friendships stretched across states, survival of a marriage weathered by distance and fatigue, survival of myself in a system that seemed designed to grind me down. But survival isn't the end of the story. Eventually, the fog began to thin. Slowly, I started reaching for connection again, both inside and outside of medicine. And in those first fragile steps, I began to realize that surviving wasn't enough—I wanted to belong.

CHAPTER TWELVE
The Comparison Game

There's something maddening that happens when you're going through a hard time. A little voice pipes up in your head: *It could be worse. Imagine if [insert your worst fear here] happened.* I call this the comparison game.

Some of you might even be playing it while you read this: *This doesn't sound that bad. Why is she complaining?* And maybe you're right. Maybe I shouldn't complain—this is the career I chose, after all.

But here's the truth: I'm allowed to complain. Because residency is hard. And the 167,083 other resident doctors in this country (as of 2024) would probably nod their heads right along with me—if they had the time or energy to pick up a book between shifts.

The system we're all trapped in wasn't exactly designed with our well-being in mind. The modern residency model was created over a century ago by Dr. William Osler, who believed young physicians should "reside" in the hospital, essentially living there full time. Around the same era, another influential figure, Dr. William Halsted at Johns Hopkins, was quietly battling a cocaine and morphine addiction—substances he originally used for surgical experiments and later to cope with the demands of nonstop work. The culture of sleepless, overworked trainees stuck.

And here we are, more than 100 years later, still doing it.

To be fair, governing bodies like the Accreditation Council for Graduate Medical Education (ACGME) have tried to reel it in. They set an "eighty-hour workweek" limit, averaged over four weeks.

Sounds protective, right?

Here's what it actually means: you can work ninety-five hours one week—leaving less than fifty hours for sleep if you do nothing but sleep and work—as long as you log a "lighter" seventy-two hours the next. On paper, you're in compliance. In reality, you're exhausted, underpaid, and expected to keep functioning at the top of your game while caring for the sickest patients in the hospital.

It's abominable.

Going back to the comparison game. By residency standards, I actually have it pretty good. Psychiatry is known for offering some of the best work-life balance in medicine. My schedule now— fifty to sixty-five hours a week—is tough, but it's not brutal. But does that mean I'm not allowed to lament my experience? I don't think so.

To be fair, this book isn't really about the relative ease of psychiatry residency. I'm writing it because of the year before—my transitional year—and the depression it threw me into. That year, I got a taste of what other specialties endure. Surgery, for example. Internal medicine. Emergency medicine.

My surgery month was a blur of six-day workweeks and 4:00 a.m. alarms. I'd trade breakfast for twenty more minutes of sleep, then drag myself into the hospital for rounds that started at 5:30 a.m. sharp.

I hated it.

And here's the kicker: future surgeons do this not for one month, but for five years. Longer, if they sub-specialize. It's unconscionable. We expect surgeons to be sharp, steady, and well rested when we hand over our bodies to them. But the truth is, in many teaching hospitals, it's the residents holding the scalpel. And I promise you; they are not well-rested.

So yes, I had it hard-ish, but not surgery-hard. There were months when I caught a break, like during my nephrology elective, when I didn't work weekends and got home by 3:00 p.m., which felt like a vacation. But just because my transitional year wasn't the hardest residency out there doesn't mean my experience wasn't real or valid. I never wanted to be a surgeon (I have no interest in the specialty and the hours repulsed me), but I was thrown into rotations that broke me down all the same. And I had to claw my way back from that—with therapy, medication, and time.

If you're reading this while suffering from depression, I want to pause here. First: I applaud you. Reading a book while depressed is no small feat. I couldn't do it—my own beloved hobby disappeared completely in that fog. Second: I want you to know that no matter your circumstances, your sadness matters. Your pain is legitimate. Nobody with "worse trauma" or a "harder life" gets to look down on you for struggling. You're allowed to feel this way. And I pray, with everything in me, that one day soon the fog lifts for you like it did for me.

Residents across every specialty are playing the same game with the ACGME, and everyone knows it. I'd wager even the ACGME executives are aware. Each year they send out surveys, tally up our "wellness" responses, and occasionally put a program on probation if enough residents complain. But that process is slow, political, and usually toothless. Meanwhile, the work keeps coming.

So what do we do? We lie. I've lied. I've logged seventy-five hours when I actually worked eighty-five. Because here's the catch: the eighty-hour limit that's supposed to protect us is the same limit that can get us into trouble. If our logged hours cross that line, we're not congratulated for our honesty—we're dragged into the program director's office for a "discussion." We get lectured about efficiency, about typing faster, about "time management," as if the problem is our note speed and not the fact that the system expects too much in too little time.

Maybe you're thinking we should have known what we were signing up for. And to an extent, we knew residency would be hard. But here's what you can't know until you're in it: medical school doesn't prepare you for this. Even the hardest clerkships are a kind of soft landing. You're shielded, supported, "pampered" compared to the real thing. It isn't until you cross the line into residency that you realize just how grueling it is—and by then, you're already too deep to turn back.

Residency as it exists today is not sustainable. Every year bright, talented people decide against medicine because they see what this system does to us. I don't blame them. Some days I wonder whether I made the right choice. Whether all the sacrifice—the hours, the depression, the constant pressure—is worth it. I don't have an answer yet. But the fact that I even have to ask should tell you something.

Let me share one story before we wrap this chapter up. During my surgery rotation, which you already know was grueling, I worked alongside a fellow intern who was a categorical surgery resident. I'll call him "Kevin."

Kevin was brilliant. He arrived every morning before me—and I was there at 5:00 a.m.—with the patient list already updated before I'd even logged in. On rounds he had an answer for every question. He scrubbed into every case he could, and the attendings loved him. Kevin was, by every measure, a badass doctor.

Standing next to him, I felt like an imposter. Not because he made me feel that way—he never once looked down on me—but because he was just that good. I admired him. I still hope that the years of surgical training don't dim his spirit, because he will make an excellent physician.

Over that month, Kevin and I became something like friends. We ate lunch together most days. And while I marveled at his work ethic, I also worried for him. Kevin gave everything to the hospital: his time, energy, relationships, and hobbies. He worked hard and it showed. But behind his eyes, I saw something darker. Kevin was depressed. If it weren't for his job, I didn't think he had much else anchoring him.

What struck me most was his kindness. Even though he was clearly suffering, he never made me feel lesser for struggling with the rotation. If anything, he played the opposite of the comparison game. His presence said what words couldn't: *It's okay that this is hard. It's hard for me too. And we'll survive.*

Here's what I know now: pain doesn't need to be ranked to matter. Residency has a way of turning suffering into a competition—who worked the longest hours, who survived the toughest attending, who got the least sleep. I bought into it for a while. I told myself my depression wasn't "serious" because I wasn't a surgery resident, or because someone else surely had it worse. But minimizing my pain didn't make it go away. It just made me feel smaller inside of it.

The truth is there is no trophy for suffering the most. There's just you, in your own body, trying to make it through. And if you're struggling, that struggle deserves to be taken seriously—no matter what anyone else is going through. I see that now in my patients, and I see it in myself.

So I'll say it plainly: your pain matters. My pain mattered. We don't need to earn the right to feel broken.

CHAPTER THIRTEEN
The Marriage Survives Too

Intern year didn't just break me—it cracked open my marriage, too. When you share a life with someone, depression doesn't stay contained in one body. It spills into the space between you. It reshapes the air in your home. It affects both of you, whether you want it to or not.

Tyler is a godsend. I met him when I was a second-year medical student, all bright-eyed ambition, and now he's married to me as a second-year resident. The road to becoming a doctor is long: four years of undergraduate studies, four years of medical school, and three to seven years of residency, depending on your specialty. That's a minimum of eleven years of your life—which is no small feat for the person pursuing the career, nor for their partner. Tyler has seen the highest of highs—the white coat ceremonies, the post-boards celebration dinners, our wedding—and he has stood steady by my side through the lowest of lows. Unfortunately, intern year was mostly lows, and Tyler carried more than his fair share of the weight.

On mornings when I hit snooze until the last possible second, Tyler walked the dog and poured my coffee so I could drag myself into the hospital. On nights when I collapsed on the floor in my scrubs, crying, he lay beside me and coaxed me into eating the spaghetti he'd cooked. On the rare weekend days I was home but couldn't leave bed, he tried to set me up for something good: suggesting a walk, a bookstore trip, an episode of Ted Lasso when he got back from work. Most days I said no. But it mattered that he kept trying.

Tyler: thank you for trying. Thank you for doing everything you could to keep me, and us, afloat. I know there were days it must have felt like our marriage wasn't worth saving. But it was. And I'm so grateful you knew that before I did.

Let's rewind to 2021, shall we? Tyler and I matched on a dating app. I won't share which one, because that's irrelevant. At first I was hesitant to tell friends and family I'd met my boyfriend online, but now? I couldn't care less. This is the twenty-first century—it's almost more common to meet on an app than in real life.

Our first date was at a sushi place near his apartment. He picked me up and dropped me off, the perfect gentleman. He gave me a kiss at the end of the night, and the food was solid. But it wasn't all rainbows and butterflies. During dinner, he made a comment that made me roll my eyes: he mentioned that on previous dates (red flag! talking about other girls!) he got frustrated paying for meals only to be ghosted afterward. I understood where he was coming from, but I didn't exactly want to hear it. Was he warning me not to ghost him? Weird.

Anyway, that first date wasn't the last, obviously, and our conversations only got better. Once he realized I wasn't going anywhere, he relaxed. We were young then, and neither of us made much money (none my case, as I was a jobless medical student), so it made sense that he didn't want to pour his limited resources into someone who wasn't going to stick around.

We made it official a few months later, and by then I knew I loved him. The rest, as they say, is history. We dated for a little over a year before Tyler popped the question. I knew it was coming—he'd been mysteriously funding my biweekly manicures for months. He asked me to marry him on a beach in Miami and it was perfect. Our parents joined us for lunch afterward; the whole day is etched in my memory. Even now, I can't help but smile when I think about it.

Tyler could never have known how hard things would get based on what our dating life looked like. Back then, we were happy nearly all the time. Sure, I had moments of anxiety in my third year of medical school, but nothing like the true mental health struggles that would come with residency and our first year of marriage.

And maybe that's why this story matters. Because the man who once worried about spending money on a stranger's dinner became the man who poured every ounce of himself into carrying me through the darkest year of my life. Tyler would've paid for a thousand sushi dinners if it meant I could be happy during those dark days. Our dating life was lighthearted and easy; our marriage was tested by shadows neither of us expected. And yet, we're still here. Stronger. Together.

I only know my half of our marriage. I have no true sense of what it felt like to be Tyler on days when my mental health caused me to lash out. Depression morphed me into a monster; someone I didn't recognize.

I am so sorry for the way I treated him during those months. But I also know he forgave me, because as I write this, he's lying next to me in bed, fast asleep. Residency writing happens in stolen moments—late at night, early on weekends—and even now, his steady presence is a reminder of how much he carried me.

I've already told the story of the sock that broke the camel's back (Tyler's sock, my breaking back). But that wasn't an isolated blow-up. There were dozens more like it. The dishes he didn't put in our too-small dishwasher. The lint he forgot to pull from our unreliable dryer. The dirt his shoes tracked across the entryway that I was convinced only I noticed.

I found fault everywhere, and I weaponized it. That must have been suffocating for him. And the worst part? I knew, even in the moment, that this wasn't who I wanted to be. But the lack of serotonin between my neurons made me someone I hated seeing in the mirror.

These days, I'm much kinder. Since moving to Gainesville for psychiatry residency, I can count on one hand the number of times we've fought. Things are lighter here. Stronger too. Because we survived that season—not just me, but us. Together, every step of the way.

The cracks in our marriage went beyond emotion. Physically, we both felt the toll. On my end, I had no desire for intimacy. I wasn't reading, I was barely eating—where on earth was I supposed to find the energy for something pleasurable like sex?

Tyler noticed, of course, but he wasn't harsh about it. Looking back, I can imagine that from his perspective, the idea of being close to someone who was crying all the time probably didn't feel appealing either. I don't blame him, and I certainly didn't expect him to initiate when things were like that. Still it was strange: we had gone from the early days of dating and marriage, when the physical side of our relationship was the strongest, to being only six months married and going weeks without sex. But even without that connection, we knew we'd be okay because we were in it together.

Depression dulled our connection, making even small gestures feel impossible. But as the fog lifted, so did our closeness. We laughed more, touched more, leaned into each other again. Our intimacy—physical and emotional—came back slowly, like sunlight through a window that had been covered too long. I won't share the PG-13 details (hi Mom, hi Dad), but I will say this: when I started feeling like myself again, Tyler noticed—and so did our marriage.

A few days after we moved to Gainesville, it was Tyler's birthday. We celebrated by going to a local golf course. Tyler is a golf pro—his swing is effortless in a way that almost looks choreographed—so he played while I sat in the cart and read my book. It was the kind of quiet companionship I'd missed during intern year: me with words in my lap, him with a club in his hands, both of us content in our own corners of joy but still together.

We headed to a brewery afterward. The sun was still high and we sat outside with cold drinks, talking and laughing as if the past year hadn't hollowed us out. For the first time in a long time, the weight between us lifted. Watching him across the table, relaxed and grinning, I thought *this is what it feels like to come back to ourselves.*

That birthday was more than just a day of golf and beer. It was a marker—the first time in months I felt like we were living, not just surviving. Tyler got his wife back, I got my husband back, and our marriage began to feel not only intact but stronger, rooted in the resilience of what we had already weathered.

Let's tie this chapter up with a few words on where we are now in our marriage: we are happy. So unbelievably happy. Tyler could tell you about the panic attack I had six months before we moved to Gainesville—the one where I cried for hours about where we'd live and how he'd find a job. I was convinced we'd end up in financial ruin, that my whole life would collapse even further. Needless to say, that didn't happen. He found a job with a reasonable commute, and we both feel content with where we've landed.

Today, our life is simple and sweet. I love my job. He enjoys his. We have our little family of three—yes, Ralphie counts—and we come home to each other every night. We walk together, cook together, watch *Jeopardy!* and recap our days. It's not glamorous, but it's bliss.

I am endlessly thankful for how it's all turned out, and deeply excited to see where the future takes us. If intern year was the storm, then this is the calm: a marriage that not only survived, but came out stronger, steadier, and full of joy.

CHAPTER FOURTEEN
Losing My Joy and Getting It Back

When I look back at intern year, the most painful part isn't the exhaustion, or even the depression itself. It's the way I lost the things that used to bring me joy. Reading, cooking dinner for Tyler, long walks with Ralphie—the small rituals that once anchored me—disappeared one by one. That loss felt almost worse than the sadness, because it convinced me I'd never get those parts of myself back.

Depression doesn't just take away your energy; it steals your ability to enjoy what once mattered most. Anhedonia is one of the cruelest symptoms. For me, it showed up as stacks of untouched books by my bed, evenings spent staring at the wall instead of laughing with friends, and weekends wasted under the covers because the thought of doing anything else felt impossible.

But here's the truth I couldn't see then: joy isn't gone forever. It hides, it quiets, it waits—and slowly, if you fight for it, it returns.

One April night before a rare day off, I'd scribbled a simple to-do list: wake up, drink coffee, walk Ralphie to the park, come home and read. Nothing ambitious, nothing fancy. The next morning, to my surprise, I actually did it. Ralphie and I walked five miles under a soft spring sun, his ears flapping happily in the breeze, and by the time we got back home I felt … different. Lighter. I curled up with my book and read for hours, and for the first time in months, I recognized myself. Even if it was only for a second, the fog parted, and joy was there waiting.

This chapter is about that process: losing joy and learning how to welcome it back.

I won't act like things after that rare day of motivation were magically perfect. It took a few more weeks of dragging myself out of depression before the fog lifted permanently. More weeks of curating my day off just enough so that I forced myself to do something, but not so much that I felt paralyzed by the tasks at hand.

The cruel part was that joy didn't stay. That walk in April was followed by more weekends in bed, more untouched books, more nights where I felt numb and unreachable. But it taught me something important: joy wasn't gone forever. It was still in me, buried under exhaustion and depression. I just had to keep creating little openings for it to slip back in.

At first, those openings were tiny. A hot shower when I didn't want to move. Letting Tyler talk me into a quick dinner out instead of eating cereal in silence. Saying yes to happy hour after work with my coworkers on my neurology rotation. These weren't sweeping transformations, they were cracks in the wall depression had built around me. Through those cracks, the light started to seep in.

Slowly, joy came back. Not all at once, not the same as before. It was cautious, almost fragile at first. The first time I laughed at something my friend said in the workroom, I caught myself off guard. The first time I finished a book again, it felt like reuniting with a part of myself I thought I'd lost forever. The first time Tyler and I reinstated our weekly date nights, I realized our marriage wasn't just surviving my depression—it was finding new strength in the aftermath.

Here's what I know now: joy doesn't just "happen." Sometimes, you have to fight for it. You have to build a life that makes space for it, even when work, fatigue, or your own mind tries to squeeze it out. During intern year, joy felt stolen from me. During psychiatry residency, I learned how to welcome it back.

And maybe that's what makes joy sweeter now. I don't take it for granted. Every walk with Ralphie, every dinner with friends, every chapter of a good book feels like a tiny rebellion against the darkness that once swallowed me whole. Losing joy nearly broke me. Getting it back saved me.

Back then, joy was reserved, almost timid. It would slip in quietly, like a guest unsure if it was welcome, and just as quickly slip back out. A single afternoon with a book, one good walk with Ralphie, or a brief laugh with a friend in the workroom were all fleeting sparks that reminded me of what I'd lost; but they never stayed long enough to feel steady.

Now, joy is different. It's loud. It's unapologetic. It's me making a TikTok about how my grass is greener because it's the only grass I'm looking at. It's choosing not to measure my happiness against anyone else's but simply basking in what's mine. The joy of now doesn't whisper and retreat—it fills my life with color, with laughter, with a kind of fullness I didn't know I'd get back.

Losing my joy taught me not to take it for granted. Getting it back taught me to let it be bold.

PART THREE

LETTERS NEVER SENT

The following pages are letters I've written as a reflection of my time thus far in medicine. I found it was a cathartic way to express myself and process what I've been through. To provide you with some context, I'm writing these pages early on in my second year of residency—August 2025, to be exact.

Dear younger me (in your first year of medical school),

I'm writing to you as a second-year resident. I won't tell you the specialty—I don't want you to get tunnel vision and stop exploring medicine—but I will tell you this: I'm happy. Really happy. My career fulfills me, my personal life is rich, and I've made space for hobbies again. I know that probably sounds impossible from where you're sitting right now, drowning in anatomy lectures and histology slides, but trust me: joy is coming.

The years ahead will be full of challenges both big and small. Today, you think you want to be an orthopedic surgeon. You'll change your mind again and again—surgery, pediatrics, psychiatry, family medicine—and every time you'll question if you're doing it "right." Don't worry. Each twist and turn will matter. Every detour will give you something you carry into the doctor you eventually become. Trust the process: you'll end up exactly where you're meant to be.

I won't ruin all the surprises, but here's a sneak peek to show you that the long nights of studying are worth it.

You'll get married—sooner than you think. The endless swiping and the string of bad dates will end, and you'll meet a man who makes you feel so deeply and undeniably loved. You can thank Arielle for that; she's the one who convinces you to take him out of the friend zone. Spoiler alert: she was right.

You'll make it through medical school—not without bumps, but the bumps will give you character. You'll fail small things you thought were huge, and you'll succeed at things you thought were impossible. And then, you'll start residency. I won't sugarcoat it: there will be days you'll wish you'd chosen another profession. There will be weeks where exhaustion and sadness feel unrelenting. But then there will be moments—in clinic, on the wards, sitting across from a patient telling you about their life—where you'll feel an overwhelming sense of privilege. Those moments will remind you why you chose medicine, and why medicine chose you.

You'll learn that being a doctor doesn't mean being invincible. There will be seasons when your own mental health falters, and you'll have to ask for help. I want you to know that this isn't weakness. It's strength. The same compassion you'll learn to extend to your patients is the compassion you'll have to learn to extend to yourself. And in time, you'll come to see that your struggles don't disqualify you from being a doctor—they make you a better one.

You'll also learn that your identity is not just "medical student" or "resident." You'll find ways to hold on to the things that make you *you*: the books stacked high on your nightstand, the friends who carry you through late-night study sessions, the dog who greets you with joy no matter what kind of day you've had. Don't give those things up—they will save you when medicine feels too heavy.

Oh and one more thing—we're writing a book. Your childhood dream of becoming an author is coming true as I type these words.

Can you believe it? The little girl who scribbled stories in the margins of her notebooks, the teenager who carried novels everywhere she went—she never gave up. You didn't give up on her.

So keep going. Keep studying, keep laughing with your friends, keep leaning on the people who love you. I promise it will all be worth it.

Love you, love us. You got this.
Ashley Kate

Dear Tyler,

When I think back to how I treated you when I was in the thick of depression, I am filled with shame and regret. You didn't deserve that. While it was never my intention to be cruel, that's how it came out sometimes—sharp words, withdrawn silence, a version of myself I barely recognized. Being depressed was like walking around with a thick cloud over me at all times. Unfortunately that fog warped my decision making and dulled my ability to show up for you. Out of everyone in my life, you bore the brunt of it, and for that I am endlessly sorry.

I know it must have been exhausting—coming home after your own long days to a wife who couldn't pull herself out of bed, who snapped when she should have hugged you, who retreated instead of leaning in. And yet you stayed. You steadied me. You reminded me, without words, that even at my lowest I was still worth loving. I don't think I'll ever be able to fully express how much that meant—how much *you* meant—during the moments I was ready to give up on myself.

If there's a silver lining, it's this: being depressed taught me to value you and our marriage with a depth I hadn't known before. When the fog finally lifted I felt the full weight of your patience, your loyalty, your quiet love. And I vowed never to take it for granted again.

You were the one who saw both versions of me—the laughing, ambitious, book-loving woman I used to be, and the hollowed-out shell that depression carved out. You carried both, even when I couldn't carry myself. And because of that, when I finally found my way back to joy, I found myself loving you in an even fiercer, truer way.

I know marriage isn't about keeping score, but if it were, you'd be a thousand points ahead. You were my anchor in the storm, and you still are. I want you to know that I see you now—really see you—and I'm so grateful that I get to keep building this life with you.

Someday when we're older and looking back on these years, I hope we'll remember not just the pain, but the resilience. I hope we'll tell our children that love isn't about perfection—it's about staying, even when it's hard. Especially when it's hard.

Thank you for not giving up on me. Thank you for choosing me, over and over, even when I was difficult to love. Because of you I not only survived intern year, I came out of it knowing what kind of wife I want to be: present, gentle, and fiercely loyal.

Love you to the moon,

AK

Dear Mom and Dad,

I'm sorry I never told you how severe my depression was during intern year. In truth, I was ashamed and afraid of how you'd react. I didn't want to scare you. I thought that if I told you how bad it really was, you'd drop everything, take time off work, and come stay with me. And while I would have appreciated that endlessly, it wasn't necessary. Tyler was with me the entire time. I was never truly worried for my safety.

Still, you deserved to know the reality. Over time, I'm sure you picked up on the signs I thought I was masking: the flat tone on the phone, my empty weekends, the way nothing seemed to excite me. I thought I was being sly by hiding it. I wasn't sly, I was stupid. And I wasn't hiding it at all. I just never said it directly. I know you knew.

Thank you for coming to help me clean out the chaos that was our spare bedroom. I'm sure it seemed odd that your daughter wanted to spend her twenty-seventh birthday cleaning out her house, but having you there, Mom, to methodically go through every pile and drawer was immeasurably helpful. After that weekend, my home felt lighter— and so did my mind.

Thank you for helping us move. Again. After six moves in six years, I'm happy to report we have no plans to do it again before I'm an attending. And hopefully next time we can hire movers.

Thank you for encouraging me every step of the way, from holding me when I cried in *seventh grade* about the stress of getting into med school, to proofreading my personal statement for residency. You've never given up on me.

Thank you for everything you'll do for me, Tyler, and our future kids. You're already amazing grandparents to our nephews, and I can't wait to see you holding our babies someday.

Thank you—for the big things and the little things. You are the best parents I could have in my corner, and I thank God every day that I was blessed with you.

Love, Roo

Dear Arielle and Maha,

Damn, we thought medical school was hard? Residency is a hundred times worse. I can't believe we wanted this. We prayed for these days, and now I pray for the day that residency ends. When I think back to our study sessions before big exams, I don't remember the stress or the ungodly amounts of caffeine—I remember the love and sense of belonging I felt with y'all. Those were the best days. Studying side by side with my best friends was a privilege I'll never take for granted.

Thank you for being there for me during the darkest moments, even if it was only virtually. For checking in on me when the days were hard, for giving me tough love when I needed it, and for validating my disenchantment with medicine. Your support during intern year was invaluable.

Here's a hard truth I never shared with y'all … on the nights when I felt like I'd be better off dead, one thought kept me tethered here: the idea of our future together. All three of us—with our spouses—on a luxurious vacation somewhere far away from hospitals and pagers. Think White Lotus but without the mysterious murder. In my mind the sun was warm, the ocean was endless, and our kids were running in front of us, splashing in the shallows. We'd watch them with lazy contentment, finish our cocktails and mocktails, and head back to our villas to get ready for a dinner in town.

That vision was a lifeline. If I wanted to make it to our bougie beach escape, I had to survive intern year. And that meant I could not die. It might sound silly now, but nothing in the pit of depression is logical—you cling to whatever rope you can find.

When we met in medical school, I knew I had found lifelong friends. We're five years in and I thank God every day that He put you both in my life. The vacation's coming—and in the meantime, we've already made it further than we once thought possible.

I love you guys. C7 forever!

Bestie AK

Dear Emma,

Girl, I cannot even begin to fathom where I'd be without our daily chitchats. I used to think there was no way we'd keep up our texting streak through med school and OT school, let alone into residency—but we proved me wrong. Our friendship has adapted and evolved over the nine years we've known each other, just like all good ones do.

During the depression of intern year, our constant communication meant I never felt quite as alone as I might have looked on paper. I wasn't always one hundred percent honest with you, partly out of fear you'd lose sleep over it. Maybe I overestimate the amount of space I take up in your heart … or maybe I underestimate it. Either way, if I'd told you, "I'm suicidal," on the same day I was writing "I want to die" over and over in my journal, I think you would have freaked out.

It's not that I kept you in the dark—you knew what was going on, just not the full depth. I figured partial honesty was better than none.

Writing this now from the other side of that darkness, I am so grateful for our ever-evolving friendship. You just picked out your wedding dress! I have so many ideas brewing for your bachelorette, and I'm already scheming our first double-date vacation as married couples in fall 2026. I know what you're thinking—it better include hiking or a really good running trail. Trust me, I've got this!

I cannot wait to stand by your side in a few months and watch you crush your next marathon. I love you!

AK

Dear Phoebe,

Thank you for calling me in March and being on the other side of the phone when I cried. We may not talk every day, but when we do, every single word counts. Our friendship has been such a constant in my life, ever since that first day we met as fourteen-year-old neighbors. We never went to the same school, so our time together was always limited, but maybe that's what made it even more special—we always made the most of it.

I am endlessly thankful for the ways you've shown up for me again and again. In college, when my ex-boyfriend broke my heart, you were there immediately. In medical school, you flew across the country for my bachelorette trip to celebrate me. On my wedding day, you stood by my side as I married the love of my life. You have been woven into the fabric of every milestone, and I can't wait to be there for yours, because that's what true friendship is.

Sometimes I think back to us as teenagers, sprawled out in your bedroom, talking for hours about all the little things that seemed so important at the time. I really believe God was smiling down on us in those moments. Being your best friend is one of the greatest blessings of my life.

I don't think I've even told you I'm writing this book. I get so excited thinking about sending you a copy one day, knowing you'll flip to this page and read this letter for the first time. I hope you feel just how deeply you are loved.

Love you always PB.

AK

Dear attending physician who made me feel incompetent,

Did chastising me for getting a question wrong during rounds make you feel like a better doctor? Did it give you a sense of power, standing there in front of the team? I wonder if your patients—the ones who trust you, who see you as a healer—would have looked at you with the same admiration if they'd witnessed how you spoke to me.

I can only imagine what your own residency must have been like to shape you into this kind of teacher. Maybe you were humiliated by your mentors. Maybe you were broken down so often that you thought this was what teaching looked like. If so, I'm sorry for the pain you endured—but that doesn't excuse the way you passed it on.

Oddly enough, I am grateful to you. You became a role model in reverse: an example of the kind of physician I will never become. You reminded me that learning should feel like an invitation, not a punishment. You made me vow to never weaponize knowledge, to never use my position to make someone else feel small.

I earned my white coat. I earned the letters after my name. Years of relentless effort went into that, and you cannot strip it away with a single insult.

I hope, for your sake and for the sake of the trainees who come after me, that you've softened. I hope someone has spoken up, that hospital leadership has taken note, that you've been asked to reflect. Because teaching is a privilege, and you misused it.

And still, despite it all, I hope you're well.

Doctor Bourne

Dear attending physician who gave me confidence in my clinical decision making,

Thank you for hearing my treatment plan for that complex ICU patient and giving me feedback in a way that made me a better doctor. You corrected where I was wrong, but you also highlighted what I got right. That balance—gentle redirection alongside genuine encouragement—is the kind of teaching that stays with a trainee forever. Because of you, I want to pass on this same model when it's my turn to teach.

It may seem like a small thing: being kind to the intern who didn't even want to be there. From day one, you knew I longed to be a psychiatry resident, not an ICU doctor. You knew I felt like a fish out of water, trapped in a rotation that only magnified my sense of inadequacy. But instead of dismissing me, you chose to see me. You treated me not as a temporary cog in the machine, but as a physician in the making. And when I doubted myself, you offered the quiet gift of confidence.

I cannot tell you how much that meant. At a time when my self-worth was at rock bottom, when I questioned my future in medicine altogether, you gave me something to hold on to. You made me believe that maybe, just maybe, I could grow into this role. Even if my path led me somewhere different, I still belonged in the hospital in that white coat.

You taught me that excellence in medicine is not measured only by encyclopedic knowledge or flawless decision making. It is also measured by how we treat one another. By the patience we extend, the space we create for learners to stumble and recover. You taught me that respect is not earned through intimidation, but through generosity.

I don't think I'll ever forget the way I walked out of rounds that day—not with shame, but with my head held a little higher. You made me want to be better, not out of fear, but out of pride. That is the mark of a true teacher.

We are only as good as the people we learn from, and I was lucky enough to learn from you. One day, when I am the attending with a team of residents and medical students gathered around me, I hope to emulate your style—to offer my learners what you offered me: kindness, patience, and belief.

With gratitude,
Ashley Kate

Dear new friends,

If you're holding this book, flipping through these pages, if you've even made it this far, you might think you're on the outside of my story. But you're not. You're here. You were there.

To Marco, Natalia, Pablo, Joey, Sam, and so many others: you stepped into my life at a time when I felt like I was slipping out of it. You sat beside me in call rooms, shared stale cafeteria coffee with me, sent a meme or text at just the right moment. You listened when my voice cracked and my eyes filled. You held space for me in the chaos of residency, when your own plates were already overflowing with patients, notes, and on-call shifts. Without even realizing it, you were my lifeline.

To my internet friends—Rachel, Alea, Leora, Paige, Lisa, and so many other wonderful humans—thank you for noticing the silence when I disappeared from Instagram. Thank you for the DMs that simply said, *thinking of you*. For every small kindness you sent across a screen, I felt a thread pulling me back toward life.

When I look back now, it's easy to see the arc: the collapse, the slow stitching together. But in the middle of it, I didn't know if there would be an after. You reminded me, without fanfare or speeches, that connection is medicine. That community, whether in person or online, is an antidote to shame.

So if these pages do anything, I hope they reflect that truth back to you—that you were not just bystanders to my story. You were part of its survival.

With love and gratitude,
Ashley Kate

Dear medical education,

Why is it that you are so unattainable for so many, such an elusive feat that millions of college students aspire to—but once you allow us through your doors, you seem intent on tearing us down? You are horrible, unfair and, frankly, cruel. From day one, you chipped away at me. During anatomy lecture, when a ninety-eight-slide deck was crammed into forty-five minutes, you made me feel stupid. When I barely passed the biochemistry portion on my first exam, you whispered that I didn't belong. During my "career advice" meeting, when an advisor told me I didn't match any specialty on the questionnaire, you planted a seed of doubt I carried for years.

You never let up. In fact, the further I got, the harsher you became. You taught me that my worth depended on a single exam score. You normalized twenty-eight-hour shifts and brushed off our tears as weakness. You held out the promise of a career helping people while stripping us of the very things that made us human: sleep, laughter, hobbies, community. You told us to be compassionate to patients but gave us no compassion ourselves.

It doesn't have to be this way. You could be rigorous *and* kind. You could recognize that students are human beings, not test-taking machines. You could value curiosity over rote memorization, mentorship over intimidation. You could encourage students to nourish the parts of themselves that make them better doctors—their families, friendships, and creativity—instead of treating those as distractions. Imagine how many more empathetic, humanistic physicians you could attract and retain if you made space for us to be whole people while we learned.

Despite everything, you didn't break me. I am still here. But I wonder how many of my peers you *did* break—the classmates who quit, the residents who burned out, the doctors who decided it wasn't worth it. Estimates suggest that ten to fifteen resident die by suicide each year. This number is immeasurably tragic and doesn't begin to count all those who have suicidal ideation like I did. You call yourself a calling, but sometimes you felt more like a gauntlet. I hope someday you realize you don't have to be both.

Without love or kind regards,

A doctor you almost destroyed—but didn't

Dear the version of me who thought we wouldn't make it,

Spoiler alert: you survive, and I am so glad you did. It's surreal to me that I'm writing this letter a mere five months after some of the worst days we experienced. I truly thought you weren't going to make it. There were days when you felt like nothing—and I mean *nothing*—was worth it. No patient, no paycheck, no dream of the future could convince you to keep going. Nothing could get you out of bed on that day off, no matter how much you told yourself you *should*.

I remember how heavy the silence felt, how each day blurred into the next. You thought the exhaustion would swallow you whole, that the sadness would never end. You hated yourself for being too tired to walk the dog, too drained to answer texts, too numb to enjoy the things that used to bring joy. You convinced yourself you were weak, unworthy, broken.

But here's what you couldn't see then: you were fighting for your life, and every tiny act of survival counted. Taking the SSRI again. Calling a friend. Drinking protein shakes when the thought of food made you sick. Saying yes to therapy even when shame told you not to. None of that was weakness. It was courage, disguised in small, ordinary acts.

You didn't need to be perfect to keep going. You just needed to be alive. And you were. And that was enough.

Now, months later, I can tell you what you never would have believed in those dark days: things do get better. Not all at once, not in a dramatic transformation, but in small ways that add up. One day you'll laugh at something in the workroom. One night you'll actually enjoy cooking dinner with Tyler. One morning you'll look forward to clinic. And slowly, the fog will lift.

If I could sit beside you in that bed, I would hold your hand and tell you: don't quit. The version of you sitting here now—hopeful, grateful, and alive—is proof that you were stronger than you ever imagined.

With so much love and gratitude,
The you who made it (*you!*)

Dear future patients,

There are things I'll never say in the exam room. Like how I sometimes go home after our sessions and cry, not because you've done anything wrong, but because I carry your pain with me. Or how your words replay in my head at night, long after clinic is over. Or how much I want you to know that your courage in showing up, even when you think you're failing, reminds me to keep showing up too.

I hope you never mistake my white coat for perfection. It's just fabric. Underneath it I am human—anxious, imperfect, learning. I've taken the pills, sat in the therapy chair, and stared at the ceiling wondering if life was worth living. I know what it feels like to believe you might not make it. And I know what it feels like when, somehow, you do.

So if you ever wonder whether your story matters, whether you matter—the answer is yes. You matter to me. More than you'll ever know.

Without pretense,
Your future psychiatrist

Dear future me,

I wonder where you are as you're reading this. Have you finished residency? Are you working as an attending psychiatrist, maybe mentoring interns who remind you of yourself? Are you a mother now? Have you built the life you used to only daydream about during those long call nights? Did you write another book? Did people like our first book?

Wherever you are, I hope you haven't forgotten what it felt like to be here—at the beginning, tired and raw, convinced some days that you wouldn't make it. I hope you remember the sleepless nights, the imposter syndrome, the weight of depression that nearly swallowed you whole. Not to dwell on it, but to let it shape the way you lead, the way you teach, the way you care.

Please don't become hardened. Don't let medicine strip away your softness. Patients need humanity more than perfection. Colleagues need your kindness more than your competence. And you—you need to keep the pieces of yourself that aren't doctor-shaped. The part of you that reads novels, that laughs until your stomach hurts, that takes your dog on long walks, that loves fiercely. Hold on to those pieces.

If you're ever tempted to measure yourself by titles, publications, or RVUs*, stop. Remember that success is not just about what you do in a hospital or clinic, but who you are when you come home at night. Remember that your worth isn't earned—it just is.

I hope you're proud of me for surviving long enough to become you. And I hope, when you look back, you're proud of yourself for holding on to what mattered most.

With hope,
The you who almost gave up—but didn't.

*Relative Value Unit

PART FOUR

BELONGING

Here are the songs of love, friendship, and home. They remind me of Tyler, of Ralphie's unfiltered joy, of late-night FaceTime with best friends, and the slow work of finding community again. This part is about connection—the people who held me up when I couldn't hold myself.

15.   "You're On Your Own, Kid" by Taylor Swift
16.   "I Miss You, I'm Sorry" by Gracie Abrams
17.   "Home" by Edward Sharpe and the Magnetic Zeros
18.   "Dog Days Are Over" by Florence + the Machine
19.   "Ceilings" by Lizzy McAlpine
20.   "Everything Has Changed" by Taylor Swift and Ed Sheeran
21.   "All of Me" by John Legend

CHAPTER FIFTEEN
Matching in Psychiatry, Finally

Maybe there's beauty in the breaking, but I didn't see it until I was standing on the other side, stitched together with something sturdier than I'd had before. The beauty didn't come from the struggle itself, it came from the relief, the exhale, when I finally matched into psychiatry.

As you'll remember from Chapter One, my story didn't follow the typical arc for someone who went unmatched. I was lucky, absurdly so. Early in interview season, I sat across from the program director at my alma mater, my nerves buzzing, when she mentioned they had a few postgraduate year two (PGY-2) spots open. "Email me if you're interested," she said, almost casually. Obviously, I was interested.

Going straight into second year meant erasing that heavy, dragging sense of being *behind*—the shadow that had followed me since starting a transitional year instead of psychiatry. Before the sun set that day, I had the offer in hand. A week later, the contract was signed.

All I had to do was survive the rest of intern year, then I'd move to Gainesville to start the chapter I'd been waiting for: psychiatry residency at the University of Florida. Go Gators.

The day I got the job, in late October 2024, was seven months after not matching. In that moment, I was given the greatest gift: the chance to become the kind of doctor I was meant to be. Relief doesn't even begin to cover it. The long, gray days of my transitional year, where I questioned if I'd chosen the wrong profession, were suddenly behind me. All I had to do was make it to July.

I thought that would be the easy part. I was wrong.

Those months tested me more than I imagined, but somehow, I made it. I barely survived the grind of internal medicine before moving with my family to Gainesville, Florida. And to those who are called to internal medicine—I applaud you and am grateful to you, but just as psychiatry wouldn't be your cup of tea, internal medicine wasn't mine. When I say everything got better after that move to Gainesville, I mean *everything*. Our home was bigger, newer, in a friendlier neighborhood. Tyler found a great job with a fraction of his old commute. The pace of life slowed just enough for us to breathe.

We stopped living for the weekends Weekly date nights came back. Saturday mornings meant wandering through downtown, grabbing coffee, and running errands together. That rhythm, that simple joy, pulled us closer than we'd been in years. Gainesville didn't just give me a residency program—it gave me a place where I finally felt like I belonged.

And that belonging seeped into work too. Walking into my new psychiatry program didn't feel like the disorienting first day of intern year. I recognized the hallways, the lecture rooms, even a few familiar faces from my time as a medical student. I wasn't just "the new resident"—I was home. Every supervision session, every clinic day, every hallway conversation reinforced what I already knew: psychiatry wasn't just the specialty I had chosen. It was the specialty, and the community, that had chosen me back.

CHAPTER SIXTEEN
The Patients Who Have Stayed with Me

My first month of psychiatry residency was spent on the inpatient child and adolescent unit. I spent my days with kids age eight and up, but the majority of the patients were teenagers. A disproportionate amount were kids who lived in foster care or were adopted—I can only imagine the psychological impact of being placed in the foster-care system.

There was one patient who really stuck with me. "Joanna" was seventeen, a girl on the brink of adulthood. She'd been adopted, along with her younger siblings, at the age of fifteen. She told us bluntly that her adoptive parents would not have taken her in if it hadn't been for her infant sister. Apparently, her parents wanted the baby but took the older siblings too since the adoption agency wanted to keep the family together. This left Joanna feeling unwanted.

Her sense of self was marred by her parents' lack of interest in her life, and that manifested as severe depression and attention-seeking behavior. Since her parents didn't pay attention to her at home, she ended up taking risks with her life, which landed her on the inpatient psychiatric ward. Joanna made suicidal statements to her friends on social media and took a handful of Tylenol prior to her mom bringing her into the hospital. Joanna was adamant that it was *not a suicide attempt*, though from the outside looking in, it certainly looked like one.

Joanna was admitted to the hospital for over a week. She had a hard time being honest with herself and with us, her doctors, about her feelings. Initially, she was extremely guarded (a descriptor we use in psychiatry when a patient is not forthcoming with sharing their experiences—understandably, it can be hard to tell your most-vulnerable truths to a complete stranger, even if they are a psychiatrist). As the days wore on, Joanna came to trust me, and by the end of her stay, she was incredibly honest with us.

Unfortunately, Joanna's situation was complicated by her parents, who did not want to take her back into their home. Joanna, equally and reasonably, did not want to go back to a home where she was unwelcome. She said that she would run away if she was discharged back to her adoptive parents. As her care team, we were left in a challenging position: we had an almost-adult who wasn't welcome back at her family's house, but who also had zero resources to live on her own. Ultimately, we had to keep Joanna admitted to the hospital until she turned eighteen.

At that point, we were able to call her sister and set up a discharge plan. Prior to her becoming a legal adult, we were unable to call her sister because her adoptive mother wouldn't consent for us to do so. By the time Joanna was safely discharged to her sister's house, I felt content with the help we'd provided her Joanna's situation was tenuous. Frankly, it sucked. She was adopted into a family where she wasn't wanted—what could be worse?

Joanna's story stuck with me because it prompted me to reflect on belonging and how important that intangible feeling is. I lived a privileged childhood and have always felt loved and wanted by my parents. As the third child and only girl, I've always flattered myself into thinking that my parents wanted a girl, and once they got me, they were content and stopped having kids. Ha! I have never confirmed this theory with my parents, but no need to crush my dreams.

Feeling loved by my family is such a quiet pleasure. I never thought about what it would feel like to *not be loved* until I saw kids and teenagers on the psych ward who weren't loved. It's heartbreaking and entirely unfair to see children who are considered a burden by their parents. This was the hardest part of child psychiatry for me: learning to work with kids who deserve the world but instead have been left behind.

Another challenging patient I worked with early in residency was a young woman named "Fran" with cystic fibrosis (CF). She was twenty-six years old, one year younger than I was at the time, and had already undergone a liver transplant. Now she was waiting for a lung transplant and surviving on ECMO, a heart-lung machine that circulates and oxygenates blood outside the body.

If you know anything about CF, you know she was not doing well. She had been hospitalized for more than two months; seeing her every day broke my heart a little bit. Each morning I'd gown up—CF patients are highly vulnerable to infection—and step into her room. Some days our conversations were just a few exchanged words, but I always tried to push gently, hoping she would share more of herself: her anxieties, her fears, her hopes.

It rarely happened. Living with chronic illness had meant Fran was always cared for like a child, never given the chance to grow into independence. At twenty-six, she lacked the emotional maturity her peers might have had, not because of who she was, but because of what her disease had taken from her. I couldn't help comparing our lives: at twenty-six, I was married, starting residency, building a future with my husband. Fran was tethered to machines, her mother at her bedside around the clock. That contrast left me feeling both grateful for my own privilege and deeply empathetic toward her stalled adulthood.

Still it was frustrating. One day stands out. After her mother told me Fran had experienced severe anxiety overnight, I asked her about it. "Honestly, I just don't want to talk about it with you right now," she said.

My heart sank. I tried again: "That's okay—maybe we could talk about your goals for the next few days instead?"

She shook her head. "No. I want to rest."

And that was it. The conversation ended before it had even begun. I walked out of her room feeling deflated. I had hoped to connect, and instead was met with silence. I wondered if I had failed her, or if I was failing at psychiatry itself. Maybe the ability to draw out someone's most vulnerable truths wasn't something you could learn. Maybe it was something you either had or you didn't.

After caring for Fran and being shut down repeatedly, I was starting to think that this innate ability was something I didn't have.

I want to tell you the story of a patient who felt like a little sister to me—my first real exposure to countertransference in psychiatry, when your own feelings start to bleed into the therapeutic relationship.

"Audrey" was barely an adult by age, and certainly not by maturity. At sixteen, she'd suffered a massive ischemic stroke caused by oral birth control pills her doctor had prescribed for cycle regulation. She spent three months in rehab, missing her entire junior year of high school. Let that sink in: millions of teenage girls take birth control pills for various reasons, and Audrey did the same. But hers left her with a permanent brain injury.

The stroke stunted her just enough that she was left vulnerable: struggling with anxiety, depression, and ADHD. The ADHD was particularly cruel—her memory and focus were part of what the stroke had damaged.

I met Audrey two years later, at eighteen, on the psychiatry consult service. She had taken about twenty pain pills after a fight with her ex-boyfriend. In the ER, she was Baker Acted—Florida's version of an involuntary psychiatric hold—because her overdose was seen as a danger to herself. When I evaluated her, she was hooked up to continuous dialysis through a large catheter in her neck, yet she looked deceptively well. She insisted it had been an accident. After the fight she said she felt foggy, almost blacked out, and swallowed the pills without thinking.

Teenagers do impulsive things. I made plenty of impulsive choices myself. Audrey's mistake was teenage impulsivity at its most dangerous, and it nearly cost her everything.

Over the course of her two-week hospital stay, I saw Audrey and her mother every day. Audrey and her mom were open with me from the start. They shared everything: that Audrey had been prescribed a dozen psychiatric medications by a nurse practitioner, that her father had struggled with undiagnosed bipolar disorder and died by suicide when she was four, that her older sisters also battled depression. Their candor made my job easier, but it also pulled me in closer. Their trust made me feel good at my job. It made me look forward to seeing them.

That was the countertransference. Not dangerous in itself—feelings are part of the work—but something to be cautious about. I talked openly with my senior resident and attending about it, and they guided me in how to manage it. I was grateful they let me continue working with Audrey. It was a lesson I knew I'd carry with me: countertransference will happen again, but it doesn't have to make me a worse doctor.

Audrey's liver and kidneys eventually recovered and she was discharged. At her and her mother's request, I was able to keep seeing her in my outpatient clinic. I was honored by that trust.

I'll never know with certainty if Audrey's overdose was accidental or intentional. But I do know this: she survived and she grew. And in the process, she taught me how to sit with my own feelings and still show up as the doctor she needed. We both made it through.

You might be thinking that all these patients are young women, like me, and you'd be right. As a doctor, you notice the patients who mirror you most closely, because it's striking how easily the roles could be reversed. I was lucky that I was the one standing by the hospital bed rather than lying in it.

But not all the patients who stayed with me were young women. One of the first men I'll never forget was "Frank," a man in his forties who'd come back from a trip to Europe only to be hospitalized with a rare, progressive heart condition that no one ever quite figured out. Frank and his wife were kind from the moment I met them. They'd been in the hospital for far too long. Imagine leaving for a long-awaited vacation and returning to months in the ICU, your life hanging in the balance.

That was Frank's reality.

We were first consulted for delirium: a type of sudden confusion that's common in the hospital. Later we were called for anxiety and depression. And who wouldn't be depressed in Frank's shoes? He wasn't out living his life, going to work, or being the man he wanted to be—he was tethered to machines, surrounded by monitors, trying to survive.

When I met Frank, he was out of the delirium but medically stuck. The ICU team worked tirelessly, but he still needed medications to artificially keep his blood pressure up, continuous dialysis to clean his blood, and his liver was failing. Over the two weeks I spent with him, things improved little by little. He came off the blood pressure medications. Dialysis shifted from constant to three times a week. From the outside, it might have looked like psychiatry had nothing to do with those milestones—that it was all the intensivists, the ventilators, the dialysis machines. But that's not the whole story.

A major step in getting Frank off the pressors was reducing his sedation. And most of the medications sedating him were psychiatric ones—drugs we had used early in his hospitalization to treat his life-threatening delirium. Together with the ICU team, we carefully and slowly peeled those medications back. The problem was, once the sedation lifted, his anxiety roared to the surface.

This put us in a difficult position. I wanted to treat his anxiety; the ICU wanted to keep him medically stable. I suggested an SSRI—one of the safest classes of antidepressants, usually well-tolerated and rarely sedating. The ICU attending at the time was adamant: too risky. I disagreed.

Eventually, we started one, not because I convinced that attending, but because the intensivist on service changed. The new attending was open to my plan, and we carefully chose the lowest dose of the SSRI with the fewest drug interactions. We titrated slowly. Frank responded beautifully. His mood lifted. His anxiety eased. And importantly, it didn't interfere with his medical recovery.

I can't take credit for weaning Frank off pressors or transitioning him to intermittent dialysis. But I do believe psychiatry played a crucial role in his healing. Without our involvement, he might have stayed sedated longer or remained trapped in a cycle of untreated anxiety that hindered his progress. The ICU saved his body. Psychiatry gave him back a little peace of mind.

In the hospital, one of the most common psychiatry consults we received was for patients awaiting transplant. I was fortunate to train at a large academic medical center that was a hub for transplants—lung, liver, heart—you name it, we transplanted it. That meant fascinating cases and invaluable learning for a psychiatrist-in-training like me.

One patient I'll never forget was "Gus," who was waiting for a liver transplant. Like many patients in that unit, Gus had struggled with alcoholism for most of his adult life, and it had devastated his liver. By the time I met him, he'd been sober for more than two years—no small feat—but his liver was too far gone. He couldn't survive outside the hospital. So he waited, day after day, tethered to IV poles, for the phone call that might save his life.

Psychiatry is a required step in transplant evaluations. Most people know about physical organ rejection—the body recognizing a new organ as foreign and attacking it, like a virus. What's less well known is the role of psychiatry in trying to prevent a different kind of failure.

For liver transplant patients like Gus, the evaluation isn't about punishing someone for their past choices—it's about making sure they have the tools to succeed after surgery. A new liver can only save you if you care for it: staying sober, taking anti-rejection medications every day, showing up to endless follow-up appointments. Our job was to make sure Gus had the stability, coping skills, and support system to give this gift of life its best chance.

With my team, we determined Gus was ready. After weeks of waiting, the call finally came: a liver was available. He went to surgery and I finished my rotation shortly after. I never learned how his story ended, but I like to believe he thrived with his second chance. Alcoholism is one of the hardest diseases to recover from, and Gus had already proven himself resilient.

What I carried from his case was a question I still think about: is there such a thing as psychological rejection? Not in the textbooks—I looked—but I believe it exists. Beyond antibodies and lab values, there's the matter of how a patient relates to their new organ. Do they embrace it, nurture it, cherish the second chance? Or do they, consciously or unconsciously, fall back into the same patterns that destroyed the first one? Psychiatry can't guarantee the answer. But Gus made me wonder whether part of our work in transplant is less about predicting survival and more about helping patients choose acceptance over rejection—in both body and mind.

The last patient I'll share with you—in this book at least (though maybe one day there will be another book filled with dozens more)— was an older woman named "Susan." I met her one Sunday while on call. Her medical team asked me to re-evaluate her because she was refusing medications, growing increasingly paranoid, and "acting bizarrely."

I reviewed the note from the resident who had seen her the day before: paranoia was the main issue, and the reason psychiatry had been called. When I walked into Susan's room, I was met not with confusion but hostility. She yelled the moment I crossed the threshold: *Get away from me, you fake doctor!* I stayed near the doorway, careful not to push closer in case she escalated.

"Hi Susan, my name is Dr. Bourne. I'm with psychiatry and they asked me to check on you. How are you feeling?"

That didn't land well either. So I pivoted. Instead of arguing with her about who I was, I leaned into damage control. "You're right," I told her. "I am a fake doctor. And you have the right to ask me to leave." She took me up on it, so I did.

In the hallway, I spoke with her pastor, who had been sitting quietly at her bedside. He told me that until recently Susan had been entirely herself—active in church, social with friends, independent enough to drive herself to doctor's appointments. The Susan I met bore no resemblance to that woman. She was consumed by paranoia; certain her medications were poisoned and that I was an imposter despite the badge on my chest.

Further workup—brain MRI and cognitive testing—revealed the explanation. Susan had suffered repeated small strokes that left her with vascular dementia: a progressive, stepwise decline in memory and thinking. For her, the decline took the shape of suspicion and fear.

It's hard to treat a patient like Susan, when their brain insists you are the enemy. But she taught me one lesson I'll never forget: meet the patient where they are. Insisting on my authority or my badge would have only deepened her fear. Accepting her reality allowed me to be on her level. Sometimes being a psychiatrist isn't about proving who you are—it's about listening, adjusting, and finding the one place where connection is still possible.

There are patients who fade from memory as quickly as they're discharged, and then there are patients who take up permanent residence in your mind. Psychiatry has given me more of the latter than any other rotation, which is probably why it feels like home.

I think about the teenager who came into clinic after a suicide attempt, her sleeves tugged low over her wrists, her eyes avoiding mine. At first she barely spoke, but over time she let me into her silence, and eventually into her story. Weeks later, when she smiled for the first time in my office, I felt something I had never felt on the medicine wards: that my presence mattered.

I think about the man with bipolar disorder who described mania as flying too close to the sun—exhilarating, destructive, impossible to resist. He laughed as he told the story, but his wife's tears at his side told the truth of it. Psychiatry, I realized, wasn't just about treating symptoms; it was about helping families live with complexity, loving each other through both the brilliance and the chaos.

And I think about the woman with dementia who no longer remembered her daughter's name but still lit up when she heard an old hymn. The science of psychiatry couldn't restore what she'd lost, but it could honor what remained. Sitting with her, I understood that this work isn't only about cure—it's about bearing witness to the pieces of humanity that endure.

These patients, and so many others, are the reason I chose psychiatry. Not because the brain is fascinating, though it is. Not because psychiatry is the "last frontier," though people like to call it that. My reason is simpler: I love talking with people. I love listening to their stories. I love the quiet miracle of someone deciding to trust me with the parts of themselves they've never told anyone else.

There is no greater privilege than being allowed into that space of vulnerability. Psychiatry gives me that privilege every single day. It asks me to sit with silence, to hold hope when my patients can't, to honor both suffering and resilience. It demands patience and humility, and in return it offers something rare in medicine: connection.

That connection is why I feel at home here. It's why, after years of feeling like an outsider in medicine, I can finally say I belong. These patients who stayed with me didn't just shape my training, they shaped me. They taught me that belonging isn't something granted from the outside. It grows in the spaces where people risk honesty, where stories are shared, where trust takes root.

And because of them, I know now: this is where I belong.

CHAPTER SEVENTEEN
Expectations Versus Reality as a Psychiatrist

I first fell in love with psychiatry as a third-year medical student on my psych rotation. It was the fifth month of the year, and I had already slogged through internal medicine, pediatrics, and OB/GYN. None of them felt right—internal medicine had too much breadth without enough depth, pediatrics felt intimidating (because of the parents as much as the kids), and OB/GYN carried a toxic culture among the residents, at least where I trained. I went into psychiatry expecting to simply check a box: four weeks on the psych ward, and then on to the next rotation.

The reality was entirely different: I loved it. I'm not a morning person—I hit snooze almost every day—but on psychiatry I was genuinely excited to get out of bed. I came home still thinking about my patients and their treatments. For the first time I could see myself not just surviving medicine, but enjoying it. After months of worrying that I'd chosen the wrong career, psychiatry felt like relief.

My introduction to the field was fast, funny, and surprisingly joyful. The residents I worked with weren't just great teachers—they were down-to-earth, the kind of people who made me laugh until my stomach hurt during lunch breaks. The culture felt welcoming, and I quickly decided this was the specialty I wanted for my future.

When I shared my plan, my mom was cautious. She knows me well—I'm someone who starts projects with enthusiasm but sometimes struggles to finish them. She must have thought psychiatry would be another passing phase. But it wasn't. Psychiatry felt like home.

What I didn't know then was that belonging isn't permanent. Even a home you love can show its cracks once you've lived in it long enough.

Psychiatry drew me in because of the depth with which we get to know our patients. They share their most vulnerable truths and allow us to sit with them in their pain. It feels like the ultimate honor. But with that honor comes responsibility I didn't fully anticipate. Some of the things patients have shared with me still haunt me.

One patient who stands out is a teenager named "Kayla," whom I met during my very first month as a psychiatry resident. Kayla carried a past so devastating that I felt my jaw drop as she told us her story. Years earlier, she had suffered abuse at the hands of her father. Though she had been free from him for several years by the time I met her, the trauma still gripped her tightly—she experienced daily flashbacks that kept her tethered to those horrific memories.

What struck me most was her strength. Despite everything she'd endured, she wanted to live. She wanted to make the world a better place. Her resilience was breathtaking.

But even as I admired her strength, I carried her pain with me. I found myself more guarded at home—suspicious of my husband in ways that were unfair, wary around my father and brothers despite their lifelong kindness. Kayla's story changed the way I looked at the men in my life, at least for a time, and I had to confront how much of her fear I'd absorbed.

Patients like Kayla are rare, but their impact is enormous. Psychiatry doesn't end when I leave the hospital—it follows me home, reshaping how I see the world. When I first chose this specialty, I thought psychiatry meant curiosity, connection, and the joy of helping people heal. The reality is that it also means carrying pieces of patients' trauma inside myself—and learning how to recover from that weight so I can keep showing up for the next person who needs me.

In medical school, I had a skewed view of psychiatry. I thought if I listened well enough, prescribed the right medication, and showed up with empathy, I could help to heal someone. I've already shown you one difficult side of the specialty—the way I carry my patients' trauma within me—but there's another, quieter reality: psychiatrists have limits. Medications, therapy, and rapport only go so far. Much of the real healing has to happen within the patient themselves.

"Joshua" taught me that lesson.

He was in his thirties, a tall man with restless energy, who came to clinic every month carrying equal parts hope and frustration. His ADHD was well controlled with stimulants, but his depression refused to budge. He had tried multiple SSRIs, each one abandoned for side effects he couldn't tolerate. Since SSRIs are the gold standard for depression, we were at a stalemate.

Having struggled with depression myself—and having been lucky enough to respond to an SSRI—I knew how disheartening it was for him. It wasn't his fault the medications failed. So we moved on to the atypical antidepressants. Trial after trial, nothing worked. His appointments became a rhythm of my adjustments and his disappointments.

Eventually, his suicidal thoughts grew so severe that he admitted himself to the psychiatric hospital. The inpatient team didn't have a magic answer either. When he was discharged, we placed him in a partial hospitalization program, where he spent his days in intensive therapy and his evenings at home. It helped, but only to a point.

Month after month, Joshua sat across from me—alive, functioning, but not well. And I wrestled with the same question every time: why couldn't I help him? I wanted to be the reason he felt better. Maybe that impulse came from ego, or maybe it was just the desperation of a young doctor who hadn't yet accepted her limits.

Joshua humbled me. He taught me that being a psychiatrist doesn't mean delivering a cure; it means sitting with someone in their suffering, even when the tools we have aren't enough. Success isn't always remission. Sometimes it's keeping someone tethered to life, one month at a time.

When I first fell in love with psychiatry, I thought belonging here would mean joy, connection, and a sense of purpose. And in many ways, it does. But belonging in psychiatry also means accepting the parts of the work that break your heart: carrying patients' trauma, witnessing suffering you can't erase, and continuing to show up anyway. The reality is far messier than what I imagined as a third-year student. And yet, even with the disappointments and limits, I still feel at home here. Belonging doesn't mean it's easy. It means this is where I'm meant to stay.

CHAPTER EIGHTEEN

On Being a Woman, a Wife, a Doctor, and a Human Being

Being a woman in medicine in the twenty-first century feels like standing at a hinge in history. When I was in medical school, the American Medical Association announced that, for the first time in history, more women than men were enrolled. My classmates and I celebrated: we were claiming space in a profession that had, for so long, belonged only to men.

But that milestone was only a beginning. As I write this, I already know that when I become an attending, I will almost certainly make less money than my male colleagues. Not because of my qualifications, or the quality of care I provide, but because of assumptions: that I will have children, that I will "step back," that I am inherently worth less. Studies across specialties have shown that female physicians often have equal or better outcomes than male physicians, and yet our compensation rarely reflects that.

It isn't about the money, though the money matters. It's about recognition and equality. It's about working just as hard, or harder, and knowing you'll be judged by a different standard. It's about how these inequities ripple into marriages and families, about how they erode your sense of self as a whole person, not just a worker in a white coat.

This is what it means to be a woman, a doctor, a wife, and, most importantly, a human being: carrying the weight of progress in one hand, the weight of inequity in the other, and trying to keep both from crushing you.

I've already written in these pages about how my relationship with my husband, Tyler, suffered under the weight of my depression. It's painful to reflect on the damage I caused him—and us. I could blame my career, but that would be a cop-out. The truth is messier: part me, part mental illness. I can't lay blame neatly on one thing. All I can do now is apologize, learn from it, and try to do better the next time depression inevitably casts its shadow over my heart—and by association, over my husband—again.

Being married while going through residency is its own trial. I work a minimum of sixty hours a week, sometimes up to seventy-five (but never over that—I'm not a surgery resident!). The money isn't much either. On paper, when you divide our salaries by our hours, residents earn about fourteen dollars an hour. Meanwhile, most of us graduate with more than two hundred thousand dollars in student loans. It's abominable—the crushing cost of medical education, followed by the unfair compensation of residency. If the United States faces a physician shortage in the near future, don't look at the students. Blame the system.

But I digress. My point is that the combined time commitment and lack of financial security have strained my marriage. Tyler works too, and even with both incomes we're only just able to afford our modest but comfortable life. We couldn't do it on one salary.

That reality sharpened when we started talking about having a baby. For women in medicine, the question of motherhood is unavoidable. Our prime years for fertility land squarely in the middle of residency. Programs allow pregnancy, but they don't encourage it. Six weeks of maternity leave—barely enough to recover from childbirth, let alone a C-section. Some programs give time to pump at work, others don't, forcing mothers into formula by necessity.

Still, Tyler and I always knew we wanted children. At the start of my second year, I met my new chief resident. She had delivered her baby just seven months earlier, during her third year of psychiatry training, and she spoke about it with joy. Her schedule was outpatient, no weekends, with space blocked out for pumping. The six weeks off had been short, but she described the experience as manageable, even wonderful. She convinced me.

I mulled it over with Tyler then shared our decision with close friends and my parents. Their support was cautious: they reminded us that children mean giving up freedoms—spontaneous date nights, carefree travel. They also urged us to check the numbers. We did. Thanks to savings we had set aside for a house, and the fact that we chose to rent during residency, we had enough cushion to weather newborn expenses.

So I committed to one more role: mother. Excited, over the moon, and terrified.

No matter how difficult residency has been, I've woken up every day with the same goals in mind: to make a meaningful difference in at least one patient's life, to do one thing that makes me happy, and to set myself up for a better tomorrow. I cling to these goals because I'm someone who thrives on consistency and clear direction. If I know what I'm aiming for each day—and I track it—I can measure how I'm doing over time and adjust when things start to slip. I come from a family of accountants, after all. My dad and brothers all work in finance, and I guess it shows in the way I love to quantify things. My uncle once glanced at my journal—complete with habit trackers for sleep, exercise, alcohol intake, steps, and more—and dubbed me a "data junkie." He wasn't wrong. I love numbers, especially when they give shape to the chaos of life.

Making a meaningful difference in at least one patient's life might sound simple, but my standards are high. It's not enough for me to make a patient laugh with a joke or refill their medication on time. What I mean is something deeper: holding space when they share their childhood trauma, suggesting a new medication when countless others have failed, or walking them through a safety plan so they know what to do the next time suicidal thoughts feel unbearable. Those moments matter. They remind me why I chose this specialty and why I'm worthy of the title psychiatrist.

Doing one thing every day that makes me happy may seem selfish, but I don't care—it's what keeps me alive. During the bleakest days of my intern year, I did nothing that brought me joy. I existed in a monotony of work, eat, shower, sleep, repeat. It hollowed me out. Now I intentionally seek out small sparks of joy: a coffee run, a trip to the library, scrolling a favorite online shop. These aren't luxuries. They're lifelines.

And then there's my third goal: setting myself up for a better tomorrow. This one is the most abstract, and it changes daily. Some days it's a tough workout, other days it's sitting down with Tyler to plan a budget, or taking batches of book photos so I don't have to think about Instagram on a heavy call month. Whatever it is, the point is progress. One thing each day that leaves me one percent better prepared for the next.

Because if residency has taught me anything, it's this: progress doesn't arrive all at once. It comes in the tiny, steady choices you make when no one is watching. And when you string those choices together—patient by patient, day by day—you start to see the shape of a life. Not just the life of a doctor, or a wife, or even a mother-in-the-making. The life of a human being who is trying, every single day, to become fully alive.

CHAPTER NINETEEN
Diagnosing Patients and Myself

In medical school, it was almost a rite of passage to think you had every disease you studied. We called it "medical student syndrome." You'd sit in lecture, learning about lymphoma, and suddenly the lymph nodes in your neck felt swollen. A lecture on heart failure? Of course your ankles looked puffy that day. The truth was, we saw ourselves in the conditions we were memorizing, whether or not they actually fit. Most of it was innocent, fueled by stress and too little sleep. Sometimes, though, self-diagnosis wasn't harmless—it could spiral into obsession, into convincing yourself something was catastrophically wrong.

For me, the self-diagnosing didn't end in delusion. It ended in an actual diagnosis.

I have always been a good student. In high school and college, I thrived on structure—syllabi full of assignments, boxes I could check one by one until the semester was done. If there's one thing about me, it's that I love a box to check. But medical school didn't come with neat little due dates. There were no group projects or weekly papers to keep me on track. Just a mountain of material and a handful of high-stakes exams. Learn it all, on your own, and hope it sticks.

That lack of structure was my undoing. My concentration slipped. Studying turned into staring. I was falling behind for the first time in my life, and I hated myself for it. Eventually I sought help. I sat in a psychiatrist's office and spilled the truth: I couldn't focus, not the way I used to. After a long evaluation, I left with a name for it—ADHD, hyperactive type—and a prescription.

It wasn't that I couldn't pay attention. It was that I needed more stimulation than medical school's solitary grind could give me. No wonder I had done so well before when there were assignments to complete, projects to present, and deadlines to chase. The psychiatrist also restarted me on Lexapro for anxiety, the companion I'd carried quietly in the background for years.

Admitting this still feels like peeling back a layer of armor: I took a stimulant in medical school. I haven't since. Residency, with its built-in structure—see a patient, present your plan, write the note—gave me enough natural scaffolding to stay on task. But I know there are people who will read this and judge me. That's the truth of stigma in psychiatry: patients are judged for their meds and doctors are too.

As a psychiatry resident I'm in a unique position to say what I wish more people believed: a diagnosis doesn't define you, and neither does a prescription. I have patients with bipolar disorder who are among the highest-functioning people I know. I have patients who take stimulants and wouldn't be able to get through school or work without them. Their medication doesn't diminish them. It allows them to live.

And the same is true for me. My anxiety. My ADHD. My Lexapro. My past stimulant prescription. They're not sources of shame, they're part of my truth. They remind me that I don't just diagnose mental illness, I live alongside it. And that has never made me less of a doctor. If anything, it's made me feel like I belong here even more.

As a psychiatrist who also lives with mental illness, I carry an unusual perspective into the room with my patients. I can't fully relate to those who suffer from schizophrenia or bipolar disorder, but when I treat depression and anxiety, the connection feels personal. It feels like we're in it together—and that in helping them, I'm also helping myself. When they ask for advice on how to navigate hard days, I reach inward, into the depths of my own experience, and try to pull out something worth sharing. My quiet goal in every session is simple: if my patient leaves feeling even one percent lighter, I've done my job.

One of the first lessons I learned in psychiatry is that depression comes in many flavors. My own version was marked by barely eating and being in bed for hours on end (without ever feeling rested). But some of my patients' depression looked nothing like mine: endless snacking, wired, and unable to sleep. That's what I love about psychiatry: no two patients are the same. In "regular" medicine, five people with high blood pressure might all be prescribed lisinopril and walk away with controlled blood pressure. In psychiatry, five people with depression might end up on five entirely different paths: SSRIs, atypical antidepressants, group therapy, family therapy, or something else altogether. That variability is what draws me in—the work of matching the uniqueness of each patient with an equally tailored treatment plan.

As much as I'm drawn to the familiar territory of anxiety and depression, I've also come to value the intellectual challenge of diagnosing other conditions. Bipolar disorder and schizophrenia can be especially tricky—particularly when the patient has little insight into their illness or no documented psychiatric history. Often they're brought in by alarmed family members, or they arrive involuntarily after a manic or psychotic episode that put them or others at risk. In those moments, diagnosis isn't just academic; it's the key to stabilizing someone's life.

With disorders that tip toward psychosis, the hardest part is often teasing apart what's real from what's delusional, especially when the delusions are close to believable.

Let me give you a hypothetical case.

I'm on night shift at the psychiatric hospital when a thirty-four-year-old woman arrives, brought in by her husband. He has to rush home to their child, so I don't get collateral history from him. The patient insists she's fine. She explains that she recently found out she's pregnant, and that this pregnancy comes with a special calling: to share the beauty of motherhood with other women.

Something about her phrasing pricks my psychiatric spidey-senses. *Special calling. Share the beauty.* There's nothing inherently wrong with that sentiment, but when someone starts to describe being chosen for a unique mission, my mind shifts toward psychosis.

I get more background—her job, her marriage, her four-year-old daughter at home. She remains adamant that she's healthy. Given her husband's concern, I admit her for overnight observation. Before she settles in I order routine labs and, importantly, a pregnancy test. The pregnancy test was negative. She didn't have a pregnancy—she had a delusion of pregnancy, what psychiatry calls *pseudocyesis*.

I decide not to confront the patient immediately. Telling her "you're not pregnant" at 2:00 a.m. will only escalate her distress. She needs rest more than reality-testing in that moment.

The next morning, I call her husband. He tells me she's struggled with depression in the past but has never acted this strangely before. She was recently prescribed an SSRI by her primary care doctor after reporting loss of appetite, anhedonia, and suicidal thoughts. That detail snaps the picture into focus: depressive history plus a manic, psychotic episode within two weeks of starting an SSRI—this is bipolar disorder with psychotic features.

Here's an important nuance: pseudocyesis can show up in different contexts. Sometimes it appears in schizophrenia, as part of a chronic psychotic illness. Other times it emerges in bipolar disorder, usually during a manic or mixed episode with psychotic features. The distinction matters because the treatment paths diverge.

Schizophrenia generally requires lifelong antipsychotic management. Bipolar disorder, on the other hand, centers on mood stabilization, and antidepressants given without a stabilizer—like the SSRI she had just started—can actually worsen the illness and flip someone into mania.

With fuller context, the diagnosis shifts. Without it, I might have leaned toward schizophrenia. That's the art, and the humility, of psychiatry: staying open to new information, and being willing to change your mind.

CHAPTER TWENTY
Mentors and Anti-Mentors

Mentors are an essential part of working in medicine. This career demands so much from us, we need someone guiding us, holding our hand, and showing us what's possible. I have had good mentors, and I have had not-so-good ones.

Let's start with the bad, so we can end on a high note. If you remember from earlier in this book, I wrote about my ICU attending, Dr. Mather, who was frankly horrific. He was intimidating, scary, and downright mean to the medical trainees he was supposed to be supporting. I quickly decided I would never emulate his style. It made me uncomfortable and had me dreading going to work—even in an environment where I was learning so much. Sadly, this is common in medicine. Many attending physicians were bullied as students and residents, and when it's their turn to teach, they pass on the same cruelty. Someone has to break that cycle, or else it never ends.

For every Dr. Mather, though, there were five "Dr. Green"s. These are the doctors who are breaking the cycle, and I am grateful for them. Dr. Green was young, just five years out of residency, and he treated his residents as equals rather than subordinates. He texted back quickly and informally, with emojis and "lol"s sprinkled in. Rounds with him were a pleasure. My depression even lifted a little when I worked with him, because he made me feel like an integral part of the team. Even though I was "just" a transitional year resident who wouldn't be sticking around, he treated me as if I belonged. He even pulled me aside at times to compliment my work, telling me he wished I could stay. I was flattered, but also thankful I wouldn't be spending another year in internal medicine.

Dr. Green was a great role model and an excellent mentor. We did practice questions every day, and one afternoon, when we were running psychiatry cases for my benefit, I made a darkly humorous comment: "Aren't we all depressed?" To my surprise, Dr. Green laughed and said that he was. He was always open with us, but still, it startled me to hear him admit it so plainly. Looking back, I think his version of depression was different from mine—not less real, but likely a reflection of exhaustion. He worked seven days on as a hospitalist, then spent his seven days "off" doing insurance peer-to-peer calls to secure coverage for patients. On top of that, he had three kids and another on the way. His life was busy and full, but clearly overwhelming.

Whether or not Dr. Green was truly depressed is none of my business. What mattered is that he never let it interfere with his teaching. He never once pimped me, never chastised me for forgetting a lab value. Instead, he consistently pointed out what I was doing well, and he made me feel like a valuable doctor at a time when I desperately needed someone to believe that. I am very grateful.

One day I'll be on the other side of the table—the attending physician with a team of wide-eyed medical students and exhausted residents looking to me for guidance. I think about that often, because I know how much those moments mattered to me. They didn't just shape the doctor I was becoming, they shaped the person I believed myself to be.

So to the students and residents I'll mentor one day, here's my letter to you (also, thanks for reading my book. It means the world to me that you chose to pick this up):

I promise not to forget how hard this is. Not just the medicine, but the hours, the loneliness, the way you'll wonder if you're cut out for this. You are. The fact that you're even here means you are.

I promise to see you as more than your scut work, your lab values, your consult notes. You are a human being first, a trainee second. Your wellbeing matters, and I will never pretend otherwise. I hope that you always feel comfortable coming to me and sharing how you feel, whether that's good or bad. I'm here for you, and I want to support you, because I never had an attending looking out for me when I was struggling.

I promise not to pimp you into humiliation. I will ask you questions, because that's how we learn, but I will never weaponize knowledge to make you feel small. If you don't know, we'll look it up together.

I promise to notice the things you do well: the kind word to a patient, the thorough exam, the thoughtful note, and I'll tell you. Because sometimes those words are the only thing that keep you going.

I promise to tell you the truth. That medicine is wonderful and brutal, exhilarating and exhausting. That you will get things wrong, and that you will learn from them. That mistakes don't make you less of a doctor—they make you human, and humanity is the best medicine we have.

And finally, I promise to be the kind of mentor who helps you belong. Because belonging is what will keep you here when the hours are long and the doubt creeps in. Belonging is what Dr. Green gave me, and what Dr. Mather almost took away. And it's what I want to give to you.

CHAPTER TWENTY-ONE
Belonging as a Psychiatrist

There's a moment every resident waits for: the moment you finally stop feeling like an imposter and start feeling like a doctor. For me, it didn't happen during intern year. Not on the wards, not in the ICU, not in the chaos of swing shift. It happened after I stepped into psychiatry for real.

I can still remember my first day of PGY-2, walking into the outpatient clinic with a mixture of nerves and exhilaration. My white coat was the same, my badge unchanged, but everything felt different. Instead of lists of lab values and endless medication reconciliations, my to-do list looked like this: talk to patients. Hear their stories. Try to understand their suffering. Make a plan together. It was like stepping into a different world—a world where the thing I loved most, conversation, wasn't an afterthought. It was the job.

The patients I met that year became mirrors in unexpected ways. There was the college student who sat in my office with her backpack still slung over her shoulder, admitting through tears that she hadn't been to class in weeks. She reminded me of myself at twenty, high functioning on the outside and drowning on the inside. Then there was the man with bipolar disorder who described mania as flying too close to the sun, the woman with dementia who no longer remembered her daughter's name but still lit up when she heard an old hymn.

The more patients I saw, the more I realized these were my people. Not because their lives resembled mine, but because I recognized myself in their vulnerability. The stigma I'd heard whispered during intern year—that psychiatry patients were "difficult" or "time-consuming"—seemed absurd once I began listening for myself. Every appointment reminded me why I came here in the first place. Not to cure everything, not to erase pain, but to sit with another human being and say: *you are not alone.* That sense of connection extended to my colleagues as well. If my patients gave me purpose, my co-residents gave me belonging. I had braced myself for psychiatry residency to be competitive or cliquish, but what I found was community. On my very first week, a senior brought donuts for the team and insisted I take the chocolate-glazed before anyone else. Another texted me after my first clinic day just to ask, "How are you holding up?" Small gestures, but they added up to something that felt like love.

The culture of psychiatry itself was a shock compared to what I had survived in medicine. Instead of being pimped in rounds until you broke into a sweat, attendings asked questions like, "What did you notice in the patient's body language?" Instead of feeling like the dumbest person in the room, I felt like a valued learner. There was room to think out loud, to be curious, to be wrong without being shamed for it.

And for the first time, I made real friends again. Residency isn't exactly fertile ground for new friendships—most of the time, everyone is too exhausted to invest. But in psychiatry there was breathing room. We lingered after clinic to swap stories. We shared memes about SSRIs in our group chat. We celebrated birthdays with potlucks in the lounge. Slowly I realized that I wasn't just surviving anymore. I was belonging.

One of the best things I did was start a book club with my co-residents. It began as a passing comment: "We should read something that isn't UpToDate," and within weeks I had a list of volunteers. Our first pick was *Maybe You Should Talk to Someone* by Lori Gottlieb. We crammed into my living room on a Friday evening, snacks spread across the coffee table, Ralphie trying to climb onto everyone's lap. That night felt like magic. We talked about the book, yes, but also about our own therapy journeys, the ways training had changed us, the patients who haunted us in both good and bad ways. It was the kind of conversation that blurred the line between professional and personal, doctor and human, colleague and friend. By the end of the night I realized: these weren't just co-residents. They were my people.

Book club has since become one of our rituals. We rotate houses, share too much wine, argue about plot twists, and sometimes barely discuss the book at all. But the act of gathering—of making space for stories that aren't in medical charts—feels sacred. It reminds us we're more than residents, more than providers. We're people who love words, who crave connection, who need each other.

Belonging also means knowing you'll be caught when you fall, and in psychiatry I've felt that support more tangibly than anywhere else. There was a week I was overwhelmed by a heavy patient load and confessed to a co-resident that I felt like I was drowning. Instead of brushing it off, she rearranged her schedule to cover one of my follow-ups. Another time, after a particularly draining family meeting, my attending sat with me for twenty minutes just to debrief—not about lab values or medication doses, but about the emotional weight of the conversation. Those moments taught me that support doesn't have to be grand to be lifesaving. Sometimes it looks like a shared snack in the workroom or a late-night text that simply says, "You okay?"

The contrast with my intern year couldn't be starker. Back then, survival meant dragging myself through swing shifts, missing dinner with Tyler, and crying in hospital bathrooms when the grief had nowhere else to go. Now survival has been replaced by something gentler, something sturdier. I have colleagues who feel like friends, friends who feel like family, and patients who remind me daily that the work I do matters.

If you ask me now, *why psychiatry*, the answer is simple: because I love listening to people. Because I love stories. Because there is no greater honor than having someone sit across from me and share the truest parts of themselves. But if you ask me why psychiatry feels like belonging, the answer is broader. It's not just about the patients. It's about the people I get to walk alongside every day. It's about a book club that turned colleagues into friends. It's about the safety net of support I never thought I'd find in medicine.

I finally feel at home in my specialty. Psychiatry has given me my patients, my people, and a sense of belonging I once thought I'd lost forever.

PART FIVE

BECOMING

These songs are anthems of strength, resilience, and hope. They're the sound of shaking off the past, claiming joy, and stepping into the person, and psychiatrist, I was always meant to be. They remind me that the future is possible, maybe even bright.

22. "Shake It Out" by Florence + the Machine
23. "Titanium" by David Guetta feat. Sia
24. "Vienna" by Billy Joel
25. "Unwritten" by Natasha Bedingfield
26. "Carry On" by fun.
27. "Clean" by Taylor Swift

CHAPTER TWENTY-TWO
Looking Towards the Future

One of the cruelest things depression steals is the ability to feel excitement about what's ahead. When I was in the thick of it during intern year, I couldn't see past the next few days, much less imagine the promise of starting psychiatry residency. On paper, I knew it should have been thrilling. Intellectually, I recognized all the good things waiting for me. But emotionally, I felt nothing. That disconnect nearly broke me.

Standing on the other side of that darkness, the fog has lifted. I feel joy again when I think about the future. At the time of this writing—August 2025—here's what I'm looking forward to most:

Third year of residency. By then, my time will be fully devoted to the outpatient setting. I already treasure my clinic half-days—the chance to build long-term relationships, to follow patients through the quieter, but no less meaningful, chapters of their lives. I imagine my future career in outpatient psychiatry and I can't wait to see whether third year cements that vision. I picture a hybrid model—part telehealth, part in person—giving patients more flexibility and me the freedom of the occasional telehealth-only day, working from anywhere.

Starting a family. My husband and I have decided: we want to try for a baby soon. If all goes as we hope, our child will be born during my third year—when the outpatient schedule gives me room to learn how to be both a new psychiatrist and a new mother. Maybe by the time this book is in your hands, we'll already be a family of three. The idea of becoming a mother feels irresistible: the thought of pouring my love into this tiny person and watching them grow into themselves fills me with anticipation.

Life after residency. My husband and I have been dreaming bigger than ever. One idea I floated to him recently: moving to Portugal for a few years once I graduate. Psychiatry gives me the unusual privilege of practicing across borders—I can be licensed in the U.S. while seeing patients virtually from Lisbon. Why not? I picture weekend trips to the Swiss Alps, afternoons wandering cobblestone streets, maybe visiting Santorini. It sounds idealistic, perhaps even unrealistic. But for the first time in a long time, I'm letting myself dream beyond survival. If you're wondering *why Portugal*, here's why: during my fourth year of medical school, I had the privilege of living and studying there for a month. It was a time of growth and wonder. On weekends I traveled to Madrid, Morocco, and Lisbon, and my family joined me for the final week of the rotation. I worked alongside a psychiatrist in an outpatient clinic. Though I didn't speak Portuguese, I was surprised by how much I could understand—through body language, tone, and occasionally through Spanish words that overlapped just enough to give me an anchor. After each visit, the attending and I would debrief, and I was astonished by how much I'd been able to glean despite the language barrier. Seeing psychiatry practiced in another country was a uniquely valuable experience, and ever since then I've longed to return to Portugal.

Writing another book. I know, I know—how can I already be thinking about writing another book when this first one hasn't even made it into the world yet? But that's the thing about coming out of depression: the dreams come rushing back. I've already sketched out titles for my next two books, and I hope, dear reader, you'll give me the chance to bring them to life.

Building a permanent home. After our adventure in Portugal, I imagine returning to the U.S. and finally putting down roots. By then, we'll hopefully be in a strong place financially—after a few years of an attending salary—and able to buy a forever home or build one from the ground up. I picture plenty of bedrooms for family and friends to visit, a backyard pool, and enough land for our kids (and Ralphie, of course) to run wild. After moving every year for the past six years, the idea of permanence feels like a luxury I can't wait to claim.

Traveling for joy, not work. Moving abroad to practice telehealth psychiatry is enticing, but I'm equally excited for travel that isn't tied to rotations, conferences, or job interviews. I look forward to disappearing for two weeks with my family, turning my phone off, and simply being: a wife, a mother, a traveler, a person. I love my job, and I truly believe I've found my calling, but I also long for the freedom of trips where medicine doesn't come with me.

When I think about these dreams—third-year clinic days, becoming a mother, practicing psychiatry from Portugal, writing more books, building a home, traveling just for fun—I realize that what ties them all together is the simple fact that I *can* dream again. That was taken from me during my depression. For months, my imagination went no further than the end of the week. At my lowest point, I could barely see past the end of the day. The future wasn't a place I wanted to go—I wanted to die before the future could come and hit me with more agony. It was a dark feeling.

Now, it feels wide open. And while I know life won't hand me everything on a silver platter—babies don't always come easily, careers don't always follow a straight line, dream homes don't build themselves—I'm learning that it's not about certainty. It's about possibility. That's what depression robs you of, and that's what recovery gives back: the ability to believe that something good might be waiting.

Becoming isn't a destination. It's not one clean milestone where you stand back and say, "Yes, I've arrived." It's the ongoing process of evolving, of allowing yourself to imagine who you could be next. For me, it means becoming a psychiatrist who not only treats illness but also embodies resilience. It means becoming a mother, if I'm fortunate enough, and allowing that identity to shape me as much as medicine has. It means becoming an author—not just of this book, but hopefully many more. It means becoming a woman who doesn't just survive residency, but who thrives afterward: in Lisbon, in a forever home, on trips that feed my soul.

When I look back at my intern-year self, curled up in bed at 4:00 p.m. on my one day off, convinced she'd made the worst mistake of her life, I wish I could whisper in her ear: *hold on*. The future isn't gone; it's just hidden from view. One day the fog will lift, and you'll see the world again—and it will be brighter than you imagined.

CHAPTER TWENTY-THREE
The Person I Became Because of All of This

Depression robbed me of looking toward the future. It robbed me of seeking joy in the mundane, and most of all, it stole months of my life when I could have been becoming the doctor I strive to be, instead I was barely showing up. I've shown how beautiful life can be when depression loosens its grip, but I also have to recognize that in some ways, depression gave me a new lens. It made me extra thankful for the beauty in the everyday, because when I was depressed, nothing felt beautiful.

Being depressed made me into the woman writing this book. I don't know that I would have had the story to tell if it hadn't been for the detours in my journey: not matching, becoming suicidal as an intern, clawing my way back when I thought I had nothing left to give. Those bumps in the road shaped me into the person I am today—and despite it all, I am grateful for them.

Depression deepened my empathy. I carry it into every patient encounter. When someone tells me they can't get out of bed, or that food has lost its taste, or that they've stopped caring about the things they used to love, I don't just nod with clinical understanding—I know. I know the texture of that emptiness. I know the way it makes you feel like a burden for simply existing. And because I've been there, I can sit with them in a way that feels genuine. I don't pity them. I don't rush them. I belong in that space with them, not as someone untouched, but as someone who made it out the other side.

One afternoon in clinic, a patient told me she had spent her entire weekend in bed, curtains drawn, unable to even brush her teeth. As she spoke, I was transported back to my own weekends like that during intern year—how I would lie motionless while Ralphie nudged at me, my body heavy, my mind blank. I didn't tell her my story—it wasn't the time—but my memory shaped the way I looked at her. I didn't see laziness or lack of willpower. I saw courage: the courage to show up, to admit it out loud, to let someone else in. To be at her doctor's appointment despite every fiber of her wanting to stay home in the darkness.

Depression also made me stubborn in the best possible way. When you've had to drag yourself out of the darkest pit just to keep living, the everyday stressors of residency—the endless documentation, the long hours, the fear of making a mistake—don't feel quite as impossible. I've already done impossible things. I survived myself. And that grit has become one of my defining qualities: I know I can keep moving forward even when the path feels unbearable.

It taught me about joy too. Real joy—not the fleeting kind that comes from achievements or praise, but the kind that sneaks up on you when you least expect it. A walk with Ralphie under a blue sky. A trivia night with co-residents that ended in laughter so loud it startled the table next to us. A line in a novel that felt like it had been waiting just for me. Depression sharpened my gratitude for those moments, because I know what it feels like when they are unreachable. Now, when joy arrives, I don't let it slip by unnoticed. I hold it close.

Depression reshaped my marriage. Tyler saw me at my lowest and didn't leave. He sat with me in silence when I couldn't speak, cooked when I couldn't bring myself to eat, held me when I wept without warning. Our relationship was tested in ways I wouldn't wish on anyone, but we came out sturdier. Knowing that we endured gives me confidence we can weather anything.

And depression reshaped my writing. Let's not forget that this book would not exist if it weren't for the worst days of my life—the day I didn't match, the days I felt like dying was my only option, the days I never got out of bed. I don't think I would've had the urgency to put my story into words if not for the pain that demanded meaning. Writing has become my way of stitching myself back together, of making sense of what had felt senseless.

Perhaps most importantly, depression clarified my sense of belonging. For so long, I thought belonging meant being chosen: matching into the right program, earning praise from attendings, stacking up gold stars until I finally felt "enough." But the truth is, belonging comes from within. I belong because I survived. I belong because I kept going when it would have been easier to stop. I belong because the very parts of me that once felt broken have become the parts that connect me most deeply to others.

The person I became because of all this is not the same person who started medical school, or even the one who stumbled into residency unmatched and ashamed. She is braver. But also softer, more grateful, more human. And while I wouldn't wish depression on anyone, I can honestly say I am proud of the woman it forged me into.

I belong—in medicine, in psychiatry, in my relationships, and in my own skin—not in spite of my struggles, but because of them.

CHAPTER TWENTY-FOUR
On Self-Disclosure

In medicine, we're taught to keep ourselves out of the room. *Maintain professional distance. Don't make it about you.* These rules are drilled into us early, and in many ways, they exist for good reason: patients come to us for help, not to hear our life stories. But psychiatry complicates that neat divide. Mental health is relational. It's about trust, vulnerability, and honesty. And sometimes, the most powerful thing I can offer a patient isn't another question from the checklist—it's the simple truth that I've been there too.

I've lived with depression. I take Lexapro every night. I see a therapist. I've had suicidal thoughts. Writing those words feels risky, even now, even here. They are the kind of truths physicians are supposed to keep hidden, tucked away in the same locked drawer as our old exam scores and failed research projects. But hiding them doesn't make them less real. Hiding them only makes us lonelier.

For a long time, I worried that saying any of this out loud would disqualify me. That if my patients knew I took an SSRI, they would think I was unfit to prescribe one. That if my colleagues knew I'd been suicidal, they would see me as unstable, less capable, less trustworthy. But I've come to believe the opposite: my willingness to say these things out loud is part of what makes me good at my job.

Self-disclosure is tricky in psychiatry. Done carelessly, it can shift the spotlight from the patient to the doctor, turning therapy into a story hour. But done thoughtfully—with intention, with restraint—it can be a bridge. When a patient whispers, "I'm scared to start medication because I don't want it to change who I am," I can say, "I've taken medication, and I'm still me"—that's not a distraction. That's a lifeline. When a teenager tells me she feels like a burden to her family, I can tell her, "I know what that feels like, and it can get better," that's not indulgence. That's connection.

There's an extra layer to all of this as a woman in medicine. We're already scrutinized more closely—for how we speak, how we dress, how we balance being physicians with being partners and mothers and daughters. To admit vulnerability on top of that feels like doubling the risk. Male doctors are often praised for their "humanity" when they show emotion; women doctors are sometimes questioned for their "stability." And yet, hiding parts of ourselves only upholds a system that equates suffering with weakness. I don't want to keep playing that game.

I know that by writing this book, I'm breaking the unspoken rule of medicine that says: "never let them see you bleed." I'm putting my struggles on paper, for anyone—patients, colleagues, strangers—to read. I am choosing to say that I have taken antidepressants, that I have needed therapy, that I have survived suicidal thoughts. Not because I want sympathy. Not because I think my pain is more special than anyone else's. But because silence keeps us sick. And I am tired of silence.

Self-disclosure, for me, is not about oversharing. It's about honesty. It's about dismantling the illusion that doctors are somehow above the human condition. We aren't. We get sick. We cry. We break down in stairwells. And sometimes, we put ourselves back together again with medication, therapy, and the help of those who love us. Pretending otherwise doesn't serve anyone—not me, not my patients, and not the future doctors who need to know they're not alone when they struggle too.

If writing this book means some people look at me differently, so be it. If it costs me a certain kind of approval, I can live without it. What I can't live without is authenticity. What I can't live without is the hope that by telling the truth, I can make someone else feel less ashamed of theirs.

I used to think that to be a doctor meant to be invulnerable. To stand tall, unshaken, a steady presence in the room no matter what storms raged inside me. But the truth is, my strength has never come from being untouched. It has come from surviving what I once thought would break me.

Depression was my undoing, and also my becoming. The moments I've spent writing this book—remembering the days I wanted to quit, the nights I wanted to disappear, the mornings I forced myself to keep going— reminded me that my story is not one of perfection. It is one of persistence.

I am a psychiatrist. I am a woman in medicine. I am someone who has lived with depression, who takes an SSRI every morning, who has seen both the bottom of the pit and the slow climb back to daylight. And I am not ashamed.

If there's anything I want these pages to leave behind, it is this: you can belong even when you feel broken. You can keep going even when the road bends in ways you never planned. And you can tell the truth—about your struggles, about your healing—and still be worthy of the title you worked so hard to earn.

This book is my self-disclosure. My rebellion against silence. My proof that the healer and the hurting person can live inside the same body—and that both have something to offer.

So here I stand, at the end of these pages but not the end of my story: a doctor, a writer, a woman still becoming.

And I belong.

CHAPTER TWENTY-FIVE
Patients and Patience

Most of us, at some point, become patients. I have. More than once.

I still remember the autumn of my senior year of college, right after being accepted into medical school. It should have been a moment of relief—the dream I had chased since high school was finally a reality. But instead of joy, I felt dread. I've always struggled with transition periods, and this was the biggest one of my life. I was terrified I wasn't cut out for it. Terrified I would fail before I even began.

The anxiety was unbearable. My chest stayed tight, my heart raced, my thoughts looped until I could barely sleep or eat. One afternoon, desperate, I drove myself to my primary care doctor's office. I didn't have an appointment, but I showed up anyway, hoping someone would see me. They couldn't. The receptionist handed me a number for the university counseling center and told me the earliest slot with my PCP was a week away.

I took the appointment anyway, but I remember walking back to my car feeling gutted—like I had finally admitted I needed help and still couldn't get it. But I called the counseling center and drove straight there.

The waiting room was crowded. A handful of students sat hunched in plastic chairs, some visibly crying, others staring blankly at their phones. I filled out intake forms, circling boxes about panic, sleeplessness, and hopeless thoughts. I was alarmed about the frank question on suicidality. I was anxious, not depressed. I couldn't imagine feeling like I'd rather be dead—how I wish I could still relate to that naïveté. I don't remember how long I waited, only that I was certain I might implode before anyone called my name.

Eventually, I was led back to a small office and met with a therapist, a man in his forties with kind eyes and a gentle manner. He didn't do anything revolutionary that day. He didn't fix my anxiety. What he did was sit with me long enough to steady my breathing, ask me questions without judgment, and help me sketch a plan to get through the next few days until my PCP appointment. It wasn't a cure, but it was enough. I left his office shaky but calmer, clutching that plan like a lifeline.

That was my first real experience of being a patient in crisis. And it taught me something I've never forgotten: sometimes the most important thing isn't solving the whole problem, but helping someone feel like they can make it to tomorrow.

Now, as I sit on the other side of the desk, I carry that memory with me. I don't assume patients come to me at their worst, but I know they might. I know how much courage it takes to walk into a doctor's office, admit you're struggling, and ask for help. I know how vulnerable it feels to be seen in that state—messy, uncertain, scared—and I know how much even a small gesture of compassion can matter.

That's why I want to tell you, whether you are my patient now, will be one in the future, or have ever been a patient in your life: you are not weak for needing help. You don't have to prove you're sick enough to deserve it. You don't have to apologize for taking up space in a waiting room. Just as I wrote promises to the trainees I hope to mentor, these are the promises I want to make to you, my patients.

I promise to see you as more than your chart, your diagnosis, or your prescriptions. You are not reducible to a checklist of symptoms. You are a person with a story—and your story matters.

I promise not to use my knowledge as a weapon. I will ask you questions, and I may challenge you at times, but never to make you feel small. We will figure things out together. That's part of the oath I took when I donned my white coat for the first time in medical school, and it's an oath I intend to stand by forever.

I promise to notice not just what is wrong, but what is strong. The way you keep showing up. The way you care for your family even when you're exhausted. The way you survive hard days that most people will never see.

I promise not to expect you to get better overnight. Recovery is rarely linear, and relapse is not failure. If the darkness returns, you don't have to carry shame. You just have to come back.

And finally, I promise to walk alongside you, not above you. Because I am a patient too. I know what it feels like to be on your side of the desk, heart pounding, hoping the person in front of you will understand. And that's what I want to offer you: not perfection, not quick fixes, but understanding.

So thank you—for trusting me, for letting me into your life, for allowing me to witness your story. If you ever sit across from me, know that I will never take that trust for granted.

Because being a patient is hard. Having *patience* with yourself, and your doctor, is even harder. And the least I can do as your doctor is to remember what it feels like.

CHAPTER TWENTY-SIX
The Other Shoe

There's a strange thing that happens when life finally feels good. When you're happy most of the time, there's always a shadow at the edge of it—a quiet fear that the other shoe is about to drop. Don't get me wrong: I'd never trade this for the heaviness of depression. I know what it's like to live without joy, to feel nothing but gray. But now, even in the best moments, a part of me is bracing for it all to go wrong.

It sneaks up in the quiet. When I'm walking the dog at sunrise, listening to the birds and feeling the world just beginning again. When I'm pouring my coffee before another day at the hospital. When I'm sliding into bed after a long but deeply satisfying shift, grateful for the chance to do work I love. In those ordinary, beautiful moments, I sometimes feel a catch in my chest—a reminder that happiness is fragile and may be fleeting.

Maybe it's my anxiety, or the memory of how depression once hollowed me out. Or maybe it's just the price of joy: knowing how much there is to lose. Either way, I've accepted that part of belonging to happiness is carrying that one percent of worry that it could vanish.

I'm happy to report that the happiness hasn't vanished yet. There are days that fall short of perfect, of course—but that's just life. Recently I saw a reel on Instagram where a girl said, *I wake up every day with the mindset that today could be my best day ever.* I love that. It takes something ordinary and makes it extraordinary.

It circles back to what I've written earlier in these pages: we can't let medicine, especially the grind of residency, trick us into saving our living for our days off. We deserve to live every day. And maybe the simplest way to do that is to treat each morning as if it could turn out to be the best one yet.

I mentioned those quiet moments when fear creeps in—walking my dog, pouring my coffee, sliding into bed with a book after a long day. The truth is, if my depression had won, I wouldn't get to experience any of them. During the worst months, even the smallest acts of living felt impossible.

On my days off, I would beg my husband to walk the dog before he left for work so I could stay cocooned in bed, still in pajamas, untouched by the day. I didn't go downstairs for coffee, breakfast didn't even cross my mind. And reading, my most reliable refuge, disappeared. For two months I read only three books—one of them a short story—when my usual rhythm is six to ten. That absence was devastating. Books have always been the thread that holds me together, and yet in that season, I couldn't even make my eyes track words on a page. It was too much.

That sharp contrast—the bleakness of then against the beauty of now—is what keeps me grateful. Grateful that the fog lifted, that medication and therapy steadied me, that friends and family held me up when I couldn't hold myself. I don't take it for granted. Every morning coffee, every evening walk, every book I finish is proof that I made it through.

There's psychology behind this feeling of waiting for the other shoe to drop. It isn't always pathological, but sometimes it can be. Post-traumatic stress disorder makes people hypervigilant—constantly scanning the environment, attuned to every small nuance that might signal danger. I don't claim to have PTSD—though I have experienced trauma (see: the flood in my third year of medical school)—but I've seen countless patients live in that state of watchfulness.

They sit across from me, looking exhausted by life itself, and say things that sound unbearably bleak: *I don't trust happiness, because happiness never lasts.* And the thing is—they're right, in a way. Nothing in life is permanent. But that truth doesn't mean we shouldn't savor what is here, now. Fleeting joy is still joy.

Over time, I've learned how to build rapport with patients carrying that burden. I tell them that the time will pass regardless—whether they spend them waiting for catastrophe or allowing themselves to bask in the sun while it's shining. The hard moments will come no matter what. Why not let yourself breathe while you can?

The advice I give them is the same advice I give myself. The days will come, and the days will go, and if happiness finds me, I may as well let myself keep it for as long as I can.

Maybe that's what belonging really is: not some guarantee that joy will last forever, but the decision to lean into it anyway. To let myself believe I deserve to be here, in this life I fought so hard to build, even if it feels fragile. Belonging isn't about erasing fear; it's about making room for both the fear and the gratitude, and choosing to keep showing up for the moments that make it all worth it.

What I've learned ,from my own recovery and from my patients, is that belonging doesn't mean you're free from doubt. It doesn't mean you never worry that the rug will be pulled out from under you. Belonging is about choosing to stay, even when fear whispers that happiness can't last.

For me, that means accepting that my anxiety will probably always be a companion, just as my history of depression will always shape me. Those parts of me don't disqualify me from happiness; if anything, they deepen it. The same way a scar doesn't make you less whole—it shows your proof of survival.

When my patients talk about waiting for the dark times to return, I tell them what I remind myself: life isn't about controlling the timeline of joy and sorrow. It's about belonging to yourself no matter which season you're in. Some days that looks like laughing with coworkers after a long clinic, and other days it looks like dragging yourself out of bed despite the heaviness. Either way, you still belong to this life.

So when the fear creeps in—when I catch myself bracing for everything to fall apart—I try to reframe it. Fear doesn't mean I'm broken. It means I know the cost of losing happiness, and that makes me treasure it more fiercely.

Maybe belonging isn't about finding the one place, the one job, the one relationship where you never falter. Maybe belonging is about planting yourself in the middle of an imperfect, unpredictable life and deciding: this is mine. This is where I stay.

And if I'm lucky, tomorrow might just be my best day yet.

CHAPTER TWENTY-SEVEN
Twenty-Seven

As I finish writing this book, I am twenty-seven years old. Being twenty-seven has been a whirlwind. I rang in my birthday by furiously attacking what my husband and I jokingly called our "rubbish room"—the extra bedroom that had turned into a catchall for everything we didn't know where else to put.

I also cried on my twenty-seventh birthday. I cried about the future and how I wasn't sure I wanted to be part of it. This was just ten days after restarting Lexapro, and the medication clearly hadn't had time to work yet. I was inconsolable. Tyler had taken the day off work to be with me—we planned light, happy activities: a coffee date, a manicure, a trip to the dog park as a family. He even took me to one of our favorite Italian restaurants, the same place we'd gone often when we first started dating. It should have been sentimental and perfect. Instead, I sobbed through most of it, and the dark thoughts that had plagued me all winter were still very present.

The whiplash from that day to now, six months later as I type these words, is staggering. In the thick of depression, I never could have imagined being here—finishing my first book.

I grew up with the last name Story, which felt magical to me as a child. Whenever my mom was on the phone and told someone her name, she'd say, "Story, as in storybook," and I thought it was the cutest, most clever thing. From first grade until high school, I wanted to be a writer. I devoured books from the time I could read—so much so that I regularly got in trouble for sneaking them under the covers at night, the glow of my lamp betraying me when I was supposed to be asleep.

I ended up becoming a doctor, which I think my younger self would be proud of. But in some ways, I'm even prouder that I'm making the author thing a reality. Writing has always been the through line of who I am, the thing I could never quite let go of even when life pulled me in other directions. To be twenty-seven and finishing this book feels like I'm finally coming home to myself.

For a while I wondered if twenty-seven would be the end of my story. I had dark thoughts that maybe I wouldn't make it through the year—that I might become part of the so-called "27 Club," the tragic collection of artists and musicians who didn't live past this age. I'm not comparing myself to them, but I understood the despair that made their lives so fragile. In those lowest moments, I thought maybe I'd slip away too, before twenty-eight ever arrived.

But that isn't what happened. Instead of joining the 27 Club, I'm joining a different one: the club of writers who became published authors at twenty-seven . It's not a club with headlines or mythology, but it's one I fought tooth and nail to belong to. To be here, alive and writing, is nothing short of a miracle.

Looking forward, twenty-eight doesn't feel like a finish line, it feels like a beginning. I don't know what the next year will hold. I hope it includes family, stability, and the chance to keep growing into the doctor and writer I'm becoming. But even if it doesn't look exactly the way I imagine, I know now that I can withstand both the light and the dark.

Writing this book has been its own form of medicine. Telling the truth—about my depression, about the moments I almost gave up, about the small rebellions that brought me back—has stitched me together in ways I didn't expect. If medicine taught me how to tend to other people's wounds, writing has taught me how to tend to my own.

So here I am: twenty-seven a psychiatrist-in-training, a wife, a daughter, a friend, a dog mom—and, finally, an author. The girl who once stayed up too late with a book under her covers is now sending her own story into the world. If you're holding it in your hands, know that you're part of the reason I made it.

This isn't the end of my story. It's just the first chapter I get to share.

PART SIX

FOR YOU, THE READER:

If you're reading this right now and you're feeling depressed, I'm proud of you for picking this up. That alone is an act of hope. I don't have all the answers, but I do have some things that helped me when I felt like I couldn't go on. Take them or leave them:

1. Medication isn't weakness. Restarting Lexapro gave me a lifeline. It didn't change who I was, it just gave me a chance to feel like myself again.

2. Therapy works, even if it's brief. Six anonymous phone calls through my hospital's EAP helped me name what I was going through and feel less alone.

3. Tiny acts matter. A shower, a walk with my dog, or texting a friend—these weren't cures, but they were proof that the fog could lift.

4. Don't save all your joy for the weekend. Planning one thing midweek—trivia night, date night, or book club—helped me feel alive in the middle of chaos.

5. Rest is not failure. Lying in bed on a Saturday no longer means I've lost to depression. Sometimes it just means I need to recharge.

6. Let people in. My husband, my friends, my parents—they couldn't fix it for me, but their presence made surviving possible.

If none of these feel doable right now, that's okay. Just keep breathing. The fog doesn't last forever.

PART SEVEN

AFTERWORD

Tyler's Perspective

The morning of Match Day was supposed to be filled with energy and hope. Instead, we got the email for SOAP a minute before the Match results were released. I remember the way my fiancée said the words "I didn't match." It wasn't loud or dramatic. It was quiet, almost flat, like she already knew. A silence fell over the room. I said, "It's okay," but we both knew it wasn't. I closed the computer, ending the FaceTime where her friends were celebrating. Their joy clashed too harshly with the grief in our apartment.

I held my girl as tight as I could, not knowing what this really meant for us, only that I needed to be steady for her. The next few days were frantic. Calls, applications, interviews—hours spent trying to find a program that would take her, that would give us some kind of future. Our future together had always been the vision: build a life, move somewhere stable, start our marriage with roots. Instead, we were staring at another year of uncertainty, stuck in Miami.

We found a run-down house near her transitional year hospital. We buckled up for a year we already knew wouldn't be glamorous. We tried to find joy where we could—our wedding, the honeymoon to Italy—but I had no idea what was waiting for us when we came back. And dude, it sucked.

The honeymoon glow faded fast. I went back to work as a golf professional. She started what I thought would be an "easy year," rotations she wasn't passionate about but could manage until her second chance at psychiatry. I was naïve. I thought the hardest part was behind us. I didn't realize I was about to watch the woman I loved disappear under the weight of depression.

At first, I just noticed the tension. Little things turned into explosions. I wondered if I was failing as a new husband. Did I say the wrong thing? Not do enough around the house? I didn't understand that she was living in a different world—one where every breath felt like drowning. I thought I'd recognize depression if I saw it, especially going through it myself earlier in life. I didn't recognize it until the day I found her curled on the bathroom floor, water still running from the shower she hadn't been able to leave.

I wasn't prepared for that. I wanted to fix it, to save her. But I didn't have the tools. All I had was love, and sometimes even that didn't feel like enough. I picked her up, dried her off, told her I wasn't going anywhere. And then I went to bed, still damp, wondering if I was strong enough to carry both of us.

We got through those months of depression together. Barely, at times. I cooked dinners she didn't eat. I walked our dog when she couldn't get out of bed. I held her when the tears came, even when I didn't understand them. When she finally matched into psychiatry, it wasn't like flipping a switch. There was still a long road ahead. But we made it.

Here's the thing: I know now that love can hold people together through storms, but it shouldn't be the only thing keeping them afloat. The system that trains our doctors is broken. It chews them up and spits them out, and the cost isn't just on them, it's on their families too. I saw firsthand what this did to my wife. I saw how quickly the joy of medicine was replaced by shame, exhaustion, and despair. And I saw how invisible it all was to the outside world.

We tell young doctors to be strong, to keep going, to endure. But who is taking care of them when the system grinds them down? Who is watching closely enough to notice when they stop eating, stop laughing, stop being themselves?

I did my best. I tried to fill the cracks, to be the safety net. But no partner, no spouse, no family member can do it all. We shouldn't have to. If we want good doctors, people who are whole enough to care for their patients, we need to care for them first. We need to build a culture where asking for help isn't shameful, where rest is a right and not a weakness, where being human doesn't disqualify you from healing others.

I love my wife more than I can say. I love her to the moon and back. But love alone shouldn't be the thing that keeps our young doctors alive. The system has to change.

PART EIGHT

NOTES

Recommended Reading

Maybe this was the first book you've picked up in a while, or maybe you're the kind of reader who devours a stack every month. Either way, I couldn't finish this memoir without leaving you with a few recommendations. Staying true to my Bookstagram roots, here are some of the books that shaped me—the ones that reminded me why literature matters, and why stories can carry us when little else can.

- *The Wedding People* by Alison Espach
  A novel about relationships and reinvention that mirrored my own questions of identity and belonging.
- *The Most Fun We Ever Had* by Claire Lombardo
  A sprawling family saga that reminded me of the strength (and chaos) of bonds that survive despite everything.
- *Devotions* by Mary Oliver
  Poems that taught me to notice the ordinary, to look for joy in dog walks, sunlight, and quiet mornings.
- *When Breath Becomes Air* by Paul Kalanithi
  A physician's memoir that forced me to reckon with mortality, meaning, and why we choose medicine.
- *This Is Going to Hurt* by Adam Kay
  Hilarious and devastating in equal measure, this book put words to the burnout and absurdity of medical training.
- *Being Mortal* by Atul Gawande
  Made me think deeply about mortality, advance directives, and what it means to die with dignity.
- *Maybe You Should Talk to Someone* by Lori Gottlieb
  A therapist's memoir that showed me the power of vulnerability on both sides of the therapy room.
- *Educated* by Tara Westover
  A reminder that resilience and story are often the most powerful tools we have.
- *The Collected Schizophrenias* by Esmé Weijun Wang

Personal essays about living with psychiatric illness that shaped how I think about patient narratives.

- *Hello Beautiful* by Ann Napolitano
  A novel about love, loss, and family—a reminder that beauty can exist alongside brokenness.
- *Beartown* by Fredrik Backman
  A story about community, shame, and survival. It echoed my own themes of belonging.
- *The Invisible Life of Addie LaRue* by V.E. Schwab
  A novel about identity and invisibility that reminded me what it means to claim your place in the world.
- *Bitter Sweet* by Hattie Williams
  Raw and compulsively readable, it explores mental health, relationships, and the messy parts of love.
- *The Hurting Kind* by Ada Limón
  Poetry about grief, joy, and the small mercies of everyday life.
- *To Bless the Space Between Us* by John O'Donohue
  Blessings for transitions—words I clung to in the hardest months of residency.
- *The Last Lecture* by Randy Pausch
  Proof that wisdom and joy can exist even when life is running short.